I...Do?

"The temptation today is to see marriage as a private affair that matters only for the two adults involved, but in this powerful new book, Mrozek and Mitchell show all the ways in which marriage is also a public good whose health matters not just for men and women but also for children and the wider community. *I . . . Do?* combines timely insights regarding the contemporary value of our most important institution with a compelling call to revive its fortunes."

—**Brad Wilcox**, professor of sociology, and director, National Marriage Project, University of Virginia

"My Cardus colleagues convincingly show that marriage matters—even for those who are not married or consider marriage a relic of a bygone religious age. The social science data prove that everything we care about gets better when marriages are healthy. The wisdom of the ages is vindicated here by able scholars who rely on research, not revelation, to make their case."

—**Raymond J. de Souza**, contributor, *National Post*, and senior fellow, Cardus

"There is plenty of social-scientific data to make the case for marriage. From Daniel Patrick Moynahan to Thomas Sowell and on to Charles Murray, all showed what happens when families fracture *en masse*—entire neighborhoods and even nations come apart. Beyond that data—also in *I . . . Do?*—this book's most important contribution reminds us that marriage can be a shelter from life's inevitable storms and also a marvelous partnership with sublime joy on the journey between life's valleys and peaks."

—**Mark Milke**, president, The Aristotle Foundation for Public Policy

"We know that marriage, for millennia an unassailable cultural norm, is good for individuals and for society, yet within decades it has become an institution in serious decline. We are in the midst of an existential social crisis that has not been acknowledged or addressed in Canada's public forum. In this scrupulously objective, gently polemical treatment of their subject, Andrea Mrozek and Peter Jon Mitchell defend the importance of marriage against its myriad challenges, promoting its benefits with tact, thoughtfulness, and sincerity."

—**Barbara Kay**, opinion columnist, *National Post*

"Marriage is not simply a 'lifestyle choice' or a useful social engineering tool. It is a primordial institution that speaks to our deepest needs, which is why it also does matter so much to happy individuals and happy societies. In this book, Andrea Mrozek and Peter Jon Mitchell provide a calm, balanced, and thoughtful introduction to its nature, meaning, and lasting importance."

—**John Robson**, executive director, Climate Discussion Nexus

"Who cares about marriage? Just a few decades ago, it was the norm that if you had kids you were married. Today marriage, for many, has become nice but unnecessary. Andrea Mrozek and Peter Jon Mitchell expertly lay out the case for why marriage influences almost every social outcome that you might care to mention. Read this and find out why all of us should care about marriage."

—**Harry Benson**, research director, Marriage Foundation, United Kingdom

"What might a healthy marriage culture look like in a post-Christian society? A much-needed reassessment of the fruits of the sexual revolution has finally begun, and with it, a revaluation of the place and importance marriage in society. *I . . . Do?* by Andrea Mrozek and Peter Jon Mitchell is an essential addition to a growing genre that includes recent books such as *The Case Against the Sexual Revolution* by Louise Perry, *Feminism Against Progress* by Mary Harrington, *The Rights of Women* by Erika Bachiochi, and *Get Married* by Brad Wilcox. With sociological data, personal anecdotes, and policy prescriptions, Mrozek and Mitchell make a compelling, non-religious, and must-read pitch."

—**Jonathon Van Maren**, author of *The Culture War*

"If institutions are social technologies that enable humans to thrive, then marriage is something like a vaccine: not strictly necessary for personal or social survival, but extremely helpful at the individual level and critical at the collective level. In this thoughtful, authoritative survey of recent developments, debates, and research about modern marriage, Mrozek and Mitchell demonstrate how all of us—young or old, religious or secular, gay or straight, married or not—benefit from a culture with matrimony at its center."

—**Kelden Formosa**, elementary school teacher, and writer, *The Hub*

# I . . . Do?

*Why Marriage Still Matters*

BY Andrea Mrozek
AND Peter Jon Mitchell

CASCADE *Books* • Eugene, Oregon

I . . . DO?
Why Marriage Still Matters

Copyright © 2024 Andrea Mrozek and Peter Jon Mitchell. All rights reserved. Except for brief quotations in critical publications or reviews, no part of this book may be reproduced in any manner without prior written permission from the publisher. Write: Permissions, Wipf and Stock Publishers, 199 W. 8th Ave., Suite 3, Eugene, OR 97401.

Cascade Books
An Imprint of Wipf and Stock Publishers
199 W. 8th Ave., Suite 3
Eugene, OR 97401

www.wipfandstock.com

PAPERBACK ISBN: 978-1-6667-8853-2
HARDCOVER ISBN: 978-1-6667-8854-9
EBOOK ISBN: 978-1-6667-8855-6

Cataloguing-in-Publication data:

Names: Mrozek, Andrea [author]. | Mitchell, Peter Jon [author].

Title: I . . . do? : why marriage still matters / by Andrea Mrozek and Peter Jon Mitchell.

Description: Eugene, OR: Cascade Books, 2024 | Includes bibliographical references.

Identifiers: ISBN 978-1-6667-8853-2 (paperback) | ISBN 978-1-6667-8854-9 (hardcover) | ISBN 978-1-6667-8855-6 (ebook)

Subjects: LCSH: Marriage. | Families. | Domestic relations. | Marriage—Canada.

Classification: HQ734 M76 2024 (paperback) | HQ734 (ebook)

VERSION NUMBER 11/04/24

# Contents

*Introduction* | vii

1. Why Marriage Is Still a Thing, Even Today | 1
2. The Marriage Advantage | 19
3. Changing Marriage: The Trade-Offs | 39
4. Living an Ancient Institution in Modern Times | 81
5. Reflections on Our Work | 91
   —Candice Malcolm · 91
   —Lyman Stone · 95

   Conclusion | 99

   *Bibliography* | 103

# Introduction

Is it still possible to talk about the benefits of marriage for our culture?

Young people are getting married later, if at all. Older people shrug; it's simply the way things go. A path toward marriage is in shambles, some single people point out, while other singles say they don't care for it, asserting that single lives are entirely fulfilling. Divorced people are wary. Some on the right side of the political spectrum complain that marriage is a bad deal for men. Others on the left argue it's a bad deal for women. A simple, to-the-point discussion of the positive attributes of marriage is in short supply.

Many of these complaints arise from a common viewpoint that fundamentally misunderstands and undervalues marriage. But perhaps more common than hotly contesting any aspect of marriage is the shrug of "Who cares?" You do you. Lack of interest and apathy reign. This lack of interest means we all, de facto, underestimate marriage today. Indeed, when we asked people of all generations to remark on what marriage means to them, a common reply was that marriage is significantly undervalued.

It's time to reconsider the basics of marriage, without layers of politics, emotion, and ideology on top. Why does marriage matter in a secular, post-Christian society, and why should we still have it at all, outside some religious enclaves?

INTRODUCTION

About 54 percent of Americans told Pew Research that being married is important but not essential to living a fulfilling life.[1] In a Canadian survey, 53 percent of Canadians said marriage "is simply not necessary" when two people plan to spend the rest of their lives together.[2] In other words, far too many young adults believe marriage is nice but wholly unnecessary.

This book seeks to equip readers with the language and logic of marriage as a social institution that contributes to a flourishing society, even and especially for those who are nonreligious. After all, religious people have other theological underpinnings to lend color to the tapestry of life. But family is an institution for all, and marriage is a critical component of family. Nonreligious people who no longer get married are thus deprived of yet another source of meaning and stability in a transient world.

In making the case for marriage, we rely on the depth and breadth of social science research. We argue that marriage is more than a private relationship between two people and is more than a celebration of love. It has an important public, community-oriented function. It is this function that is rarely considered, and it is this public side to which we want to draw attention.

We have examined marriage for nearly twenty years, and our concern is that as attitudes and practices around marriage have shifted, the logic and language of marriage is fading from collective memory. Today marriage is largely understood as a private relationship between two people, centered on individual happiness, personal fulfillment, and romanticized ideas of love. While healthy marriages can include these things, marriage has a greater, deeper meaning and purpose. Marriage is a public good, and now more than ever North Americans need to reimagine what a healthy marriage culture could look like in a pluralistic society.

Moving beyond empty slogans about marriage or Hallmark-esque platitudes, we invite you to step beyond the cultural apathy around marriage and into a robust discussion about this venerable institution. We do not pine for a mythical golden age of marriage

1. Horowitz et al., "Marriage and Cohabitation," 12.
2. Angus Reid Institute, "I Don't," para. 4.

and family—there has never been such an age—but we do believe now is a critical moment to reimagine what marriage *still* means for the wider society and the communities we live in.

## The Power of Personal Experience . . . and Seeing Beyond It

Everyone has an opinion on family. How we feel about the topic is influenced by our own experiences. If we grew up in a happy home with parents in a healthy marriage, we are more prone to think positively about marriage and family. If our experience with family life was painful, we are often more cautious. Ultimately, our opinion on marriage and whether marriage is an overall good is shaped by our personal experience.

While lack of interest and apathy about marriage make up a significant part of the public attitude on marriage, obviously some people are wary of it for other reasons. For some people it's not so much that they've passed on marriage but that they feel it's passed on them. Traversing modern dating culture is a minefield filled with indecency and a lack of connection. No dating culture means meeting and making a partnership of any kind is much more difficult. Navigating relationships, finishing school, finding secure and consistent employment, the cost of living, attempts to buy a place to live—all of this makes marriage feel like a mirage shimmering somewhere far away, unattainable even as you attempt to travel toward it. Put simply, marriage is out of reach.

Others are wary because they have grown up in homes with bad marriages, whether ones that lasted or broke up. These people are living the fallout of troubled marriages. Even the adult children of divorce suffer consequences, leading some to ask why they should take the risk.

Still others are informed about marriage but nonetheless question the relevance and purpose of marriage because the foundations of marriage feel suspect. The college educated will not likely have escaped a particular spin on marriage, presenting it as a catastrophe with little benefit to anyone, particularly women.

*INTRODUCTION*

We can't categorize every misgiving. Yet even as we can see (and respect) the varying approaches people take toward marriage, and for different reasons, one consistent point remains. People continue to long for love, companionship, stability, and romantic partnership. Even if we question whether marriage is the ultimate expression of this kind of partnership, the idea of partnering up in life remains desirable for most people. Social pressure and stigma around whom we love and how we form relationships has certainly receded. In theory at least, this means many more people are free to pursue meaningful relationships. Yet without marriage as the goal, serial monogamy becomes more common than we care to admit. The longer we take to partner up, the more we end up asking questions about the relevance of marriage for today. It's something of a circular argument—fewer, later marriages leads to more questions about marriage, and more questions about marriages leads to fewer happy marriages.

Perhaps we have painted too grim a picture. It's not all bad news. The decline in marriage can be overstated. Married couples remain the most common family form across North America. Neither are divorce rates quite as high as we are told. North Americans are still getting married, even if later, even if stratified by class. Unfortunately, many of those who are happily married and enjoying stable marriages miss the opportunity to champion marriage and the positive impact these stable partnerships have on communities.

Without discounting the value of personal experience, we invite you to reconsider imagining a healthy marriage culture with us—what its purpose is and how it still matters today, especially outside your own personal experience.

## The Caveats

Before we begin, there are a few important notes about our approach to thinking about marriage in this concise primer.

First, we do not hold a saccharine, yesteryear view of marriage, one that heralds all versions of marriage over time and place as a grand success. Neither do we aim to convince everyone to get married. We don't believe marriage ought to be compulsory, and we don't condemn people who do not get married or think they live lesser lives. Yet for those who desire partnership and/or children, the path to marriage ought not be quite so muddled, difficult, or perceived as unnecessary. It's especially important for those who desire children to understand marriage is fundamental to their family's success.

Second, we are convinced by the social science research suggesting that a good marriage encourages health, wellness, and happiness. Yet we also recognize that some marriages are unsafe. We recognize that divorce is sometimes necessary, and we do not desire to adjudicate any particular divorce. Even so, while divorce is often necessary, it remains emotionally difficult. Our hope lies in a marriage culture where the recourse to divorce is less common, because supportive community helps struggling marriages grow healthier. Our hope lies in a marriage culture where we seek to restore relationships wherever possible, not to prolong pain but precisely because divorce is painful. Our hope also lies in those who feel like they're on the road toward divorce reaching out for support before the die is cast. The end result of this cultural change would not be people trapped in bad marriages but rather more people living out happy ones.

Third, while we come to the topic of marriage as Christians, we do not make theological arguments in this book. We are not putting our faith aside, but rather we are using a different pool of sources. Certainly, Christianity values marriage, as do all major religions. It would be naïve to think that in North America, Christian religiosity has not influenced cultural notions about marriage. It's often parachurch organizations and places of worship that offer premarital and marriage counseling. At the same time, there are and always have been competing visions of marriage, even within Christendom. We do not address these theological differences within Christianity (or outside it) but instead seek to promote understanding of the common elements of marriage for the public good. Our intent is to invite readers to imagine that

*INTRODUCTION*

marriage is an important public good, especially in a pluralistic society like North America.

Fourth, we recognize a range of scholarly views on marriage. The study of the meaning and importance of marriage is ongoing, and scholars come to differing conclusions about the value of, purpose for, and place for marriage in different places and time periods. In general, we think that historically, as today, marriage holds important meaning and purpose for both men and women. However, we welcome good-faith dissent because we believe the conversation is worth having.

Finally, you'll notice that we provide data from the United States and Canada and defer to the shorthand "North America" when addressing trends common to both countries. At the same time, despite cultural overlap between the two countries, there are some distinct nuances around the beliefs and practices of marriage. This is particularly interesting given geographic proximity and cultural similarities in other areas. For example, some social trends in the Canadian province of Quebec are distinct from the rest of North America. This province has witnessed a dramatic decline in marriage—so dramatic that the Canadian marriage rate increases when removing the Quebec rate from national data. And the portion of cohabiting relationships there is now the highest in the G7. We'll discuss this situation to glean insights gained by observing the nuances among regions.

Wherever you are on life's journey, long married, divorced, considering marriage, unable to get married, or deliberately opting out, we hope you'll come along to read about the significant difference marriage makes not only for ourselves but mainly for the communities and culture we share. This is a book that aims to offer learning, not judgment, for the varying life circumstances in which we all find ourselves, often through no fault of our own. We write not as a hat tip to tradition for tradition's sake but rather so that we all might understand why our world would be a better place with more good marriages in it.

In chapter 1, we explore why marriage still matters. We differentiate between the soulmate model of marriage that prioritizes individual needs and fulfillment, and the institutional model that prioritizes cooperation and constraint to benefit both adults and children. We identify the key components of marriage that make it a unique relationship.

We are convinced that the weight of social science research shows that healthy marriages are good for men, women, and children. In chapter 2 we look at the evidence for the marriage advantage in health, happiness, and other social outcomes.

Social institutions like marriage evolve, yet the essential elements need to remain. In chapter 3 we explore the forces that have stretched and pulled at marriage, and we consider the trade-offs that come with change.

In chapter 4 we consider what living the ancient institution of marriage could look like in contemporary life. We argue there is much work to be done to forge a healthy marriage culture, and we consider where civil society and public policy could best support the growth of a robust marriage culture.

Our desire is to foster a public conversation about marriage and its relevance in society. Chapter 5 features two responses. First a thoughtful, personal reflection that invites consideration for the practical ramification of contemporary marriage culture from Canadian journalist and media entrepreneur Candice Malcolm. Then American demographer and policy expert Lyman Stone identifies what it will take to shape a thriving marriage culture.

## Public Opinion on Marriage

There was a time not so long ago when our relationships and dating lives were still oriented toward marriage. In the 1970s, De Beers Jewelry ran an ad in *Seventeen* magazine, of all places. The idea that a diamond company would market engagement and marriage to their teenage readership now seems quaint, crazy, even dangerous. But even as they did so, the status of marriage was changing. Above the familiar tagline "Diamonds are forever," the script reads, "I know to the world it says we're getting married. But to me, it says why." Marriage had already become a personal affair, not merely a socially expected progression toward adulthood. The words "to me" signal an individual, personalized justification.

Today, the diamond industry has altered course dramatically. To successfully market diamonds to young adults, the industry believes it needs to maintain the marriage between diamonds and romantic love, while divorcing the product (pardon the puns) from the promise of matrimony. A recent Diamond Producers Association ad campaign aimed at young adults used the slogan "Real Is Rare." The online advertising spots display fast-paced, emotionally charged images of passion intertwined with images of intense relational conflict. In one advertisement, a voice-over says, "Maybe we'll never get married." And in examining the data, it would seem the diamond industry knows the social trends. Increasingly, young adults are not marrying, and if they do, they are tying the knot at later ages than in the past.

Over the last half century, the decline of marriage has been central to the story of family change. In 1971, for instance, married couples accounted for 91 percent of census families in Canada. Today, the portion of married couples has fallen to 65 percent. The decline in marriage has been accompanied by a rise in living common law, which has tripled from 6 percent in 1981 to 19 percent by 2021. Unsurprisingly, attitudes toward marriage also shifted dramatically during the 1970s. A Gallup survey found that approval for living together before marriage jumped 22 percent among young adults during the first half of the 1970s.[3]

The United States has also witnessed a dramatic decline in marriage over the last number of decades. US data suggest that the marriage rate among women declined nearly 60 percent from 1970 to 2010.[4] The result is that the number of children living with two parents has declined from about 85 percent to 70 percent over the last fifty years.[5]

---

3. Canadian Institute of Public Opinion, "Under Thirty, Trial Marriages"; "Majority, under Thirty, Approve."

4. Cruz, *Marriage*.

5. Hemez and Washington, "Percentage and Number of Children."

## INTRODUCTION

With diamond companies, education programs, and even many places of worship no longer pointing toward marriage, you might think that people have soured on this family form. In fact, both Americans and Canadians are not so much negative about marriage as they are uninterested.

In a 2016 survey, 72 percent of Canadians aged eighteen to twenty-nine viewed marriage as a positive or somewhat positive aspect of family life.[6] A significant majority of young adults hold positive views about marriage but view the family form as one option among an array of choices. In a 2018 survey, 53 percent of Canadians said marriage "is simply not necessary" when two people plan to spend the rest of their lives together.[7] In short, North American adults believe marriage is nice but unnecessary.

The shifting permissive attitudes around living together outside marriage since the 1970s mean young adults experience fewer social constraints around their partnership decisions. Even so, marriage retains its status as a significant commitment. Data from the Canadian 2017 General Social Survey reveal that the primary motivation to marry among currently married young adults aged twenty-five to thirty-four was proof of love and commitment. Cultural, moral, and religious reasons were the second most cited influence for getting married.[8] A similar survey found that among American adults, love and companionship were the top reasons for couples to marry, followed by the desire for a formal commitment.[9]

The desire for greater commitment is a significant personal motivation to marry, but cultural and religious influences remain a compelling force in the decision. Marriage is an institution that thrives when supported by other institutions. Our views of marriage are shaped by cultural influences.

Our cultural value of individualism has shaped how we understand marriage as a personal good. The idea that marriage is an

6. Mitchell, *Canadian Millennials and Value.*
7. Angus Reid Institute, "I Don't," para. 4.
8. Mitchell and Day, "For Love or Money?"
9. Horowitz et al., "Marriage and Cohabitation," 31.

institution that contributes to the public good may sound strange to many young adults. In 2016 a quarter of younger Canadians were more likely than their elders to agree that marriage is an outdated institution. Since Canadians were last asked the same question twenty years earlier, opinions have shifted toward a neutral position, with about one in five neither agreeing nor disagreeing that marriage is an outdated institution.[10]

Marriage may not be outdated, but many Americans believe the family form is moving in that direction. Pew Research reported in 2019 that about 43 percent of American adults agree that the institution of marriage has become obsolete.[11] This may speak to how individualism has shaped attitudes toward the public function of marriage.

What we know with certainty is that attitudes toward the marriage commitment have shifted significantly since the 1970s. Young adults generally remain positive about marriage even as they consider it one option among many. They think of marriage in personal terms with less consideration, or perhaps less knowledge, of the institution's public function. Married couples make up a significant portion of families. Yet fewer marriages may be a self-fulfilling prophecy as fewer examples of healthy marriage are visible as a cultural guidepost.

---

10. Mitchell, *Canadian Millennials and Value*.
11. Horowitz et al., "Marriage and Cohabitation," 29.

# 1

# Why Marriage Is Still a Thing, Even Today

THE PUBLIC OPINION DATA on marriage shows that people are not opposed to the idea of marriage, but neither are they terribly passionate about it. Marriage has simply become optional in family life. Later, in chapter 3, we explore the social trends and forces that have pulled and stretched marriage, shifting how many people think about and practice marriage. Now in this first chapter, we make the positive case for marriage, understanding that we already live in a world where we are living out the consequences of its decline.

The decline in marriage and resulting family instability have contributed to social challenges facing our communities such as isolation, poverty, and declining health and happiness. Observable challenges such as food and housing insecurity are an indicator of economic poverty. Yet declining health and happiness reveal a kind of spiritual poverty—often a factor in economic poverty. Loneliness and isolation, symptoms of spiritual poverty, can be more difficult to diagnose, making it more challenging to find and discuss solutions. Family, including marriage, is a factor in both forms of poverty rarely considered by policymakers when confronting daunting social challenges. We can no longer ignore marriage and family. According to Nobel Laureate economist James Heckman, "Nobody wants to talk about the family, and the family's the whole story.... And it's the whole story about a lot of social and economic issues."[1]

If family is the whole story, then it should be a factor in responding to rising rates of isolation. Take a recent, and sadly all too common, example of a particular form of poverty in North America. The mayor of a small Canadian border town called for a state of emergency after seventeen people overdosed in less than twenty-four hours. This tragedy is a form of poverty, borne out in part because of disconnection. While the causes of the drug epidemic are complex, the loss of robust family safety nets is a contributing factor. We know this to be the case with underhoused people. A number of studies have found that family disruption is a common experience among those experiencing homelessness.[2] The portion of underhoused people would be much higher without family safety nets. Augsburg University scholar Timothy Pippert observes, "The most important and effective social institution at keeping its members from living on the street is the family. Family safety nets of financial and emotional support are what keep the ranks of the homeless from exploding on a daily basis."[3] Family cannot be ignored.

Of course, drug abuse is a multifaceted problem that includes various economic and social factors. There is evidence to suggest that family instability, including changes in family structure like divorce, are correlated with increased risk for youth substance abuse.[4] Having volunteered and become friends with young people in the child welfare system, I (Andrea) have become sadly familiar with the ways in which family instability is a factor to be

---

1. Heckman, "Role of Families," 32:55.
2. Caton et al., "Risk Factors for Homelessness"; Lee and Schreck, "Danger on the Streets"; Koegel et al., "Childhood Risk Factors"; Herman et al., "Adverse Childhood Experiences."
3. Pippert, *Road Dogs and Loners*, 64.
4. Thornberry et al., "Family Disruption and Delinquency."

reckoned with in these friends' lives. There are no simple answers; certainly not all marriages are healthy and safe, nor are married couples always able to withstand addictions and other destructive behaviors. But for the kids and young adults I've come to know, healthy marriage is frequently absent in their lives going back two generations. There is much evidence in support of the protective power of two parents, yet depending on where we live, we rarely talk about this.[5] I always feel a twinge of its absence in so many of the training courses geared toward youth and young adults in the child welfare system. My mind has certainly wandered toward the big questions—how do we increase family stability and strengthen the capacity of families to raise their children? After all, the key problem with youth sleeping on the streets certainly isn't that they have a safe and secure home life behind them. Rather, more often than not, they are escaping a broken home life.

Although significant social problems such as the opioid overdose epidemic seem unrelated to marriage, we have come to wonder what role family stability plays and whether a reimagined perspective on marriage—agreement that marriage matters—would offer a positive contribution.

One of the people we interviewed for this book, Rebecca, a thirty-five-year-old from the East Coast of Canada, put it this way in considering the value of marriage in community: "Marriage . . . allows for more connection time between parent and child. It empowers parents to use their authority as a united front. And marriage allows for more connection time for adults overall. I think a return to strengthened human connection would solve a lot of the cultural problems we face."

The deficit in deep relationships—both marital and friendship—has become particularly evident in our cultural moment. The trend toward "bowling alone," as Robert Putnam put it in the title of his landmark book, is very clear. People belong to associations of civil society less; they go to sports clubs, rotary clubs, business associations, places of worship, women's and men's clubs, charities—less. More adults are living alone. As we have

5. Kearney, *Two-Parent Privilege*.

witnessed in our home country of Canada, the portion of adults in their twenties and early thirties (prime marrying age) who are partnered has declined.[6] This development mirrors the trends Putnam observed. Did this loneliness start with the decline in marriage? It's hard to say. Certainly, we are in a spiral, living out atomized lives with little stability. We move often for work. Work communities become primary communities—the place we spend all our time. But work also shifts and changes. The idea of staying at one workplace for a lifetime is laughable and, more importantly, impossible, even were it desired.

Marriage is one of the last remaining places where, for as often as we fail, we consider a partnership between two people to last until death. As we marry later or not at all, we have a growing mass of people for whom marriage is not necessary simply because they've chosen not to do it.

Outside religious communities, where marriage is emphasized and valued as a norm, we lack an end goal toward which to steer our relationships. Nice but unnecessary means people partnering up for shorter times, living in a holding pattern for longer, and not experiencing the benefits of full commitment. Again, while this relationship is not causal, as marriage becomes a less obvious and less necessary choice, and people increasingly fail to see marriage as an end point for relationship, dating culture also suffers. How else can apps that pitch short-term flings survive and thrive? As the plethora of opportunities to "connect" (we use that word loosely as it pertains to online dating) increase, they are doing so in a climate that does not nurture or encourage real, long-lasting connection. A culture that has lost the vocabulary for presenting marriage as a good isn't effectively providing a path to achieve long-lasting connection. Yet many still want this kind of connection, and marriage is the gold standard for it.

As a result, dating culture collapses, creating a circular effect: the collapse of marriage culture changes dating culture, and a lack of dating culture diminishes the possibility of a marriage culture.

---

6. Mitchell, "Living La Vida Lonely."

People who never meet cannot get married, and so dating, too, needs to be restored alongside marriage.

Consider what marriage offers that other relationships do not: bringing together two people without a blood relationship into a community of their own creation through family life. Children learn how to live in the world by watching their parents, who have a better chance of remaining together and enduring bad times when married. We believe the shift in North America toward viewing marriage as nice but unnecessary is resulting in fewer people who consider the benefits of marriage and its impact on communities.

## You Complete Me: The Soulmate Model of Marriage

The shift in marital patterns over the last half century or so toward fewer people marrying, and those who marry doing so at later ages, has unfolded in a culture that is becoming hyper-individualized. We differentiate between two broad models: the soulmate marriage, which is more inward facing, and the institutional model. The former is the dominant understanding of marriage today. The latter, the institutional model, is far more robust but less commonly understood.

In the classic scene from the 1996 film *Jerry Maguire*, Tom Cruise's character confesses his love to Dorothy (played by Renée Zellweger). In the meme-worthy moment, Cruise breathlessly says, "You . . ." pausing for dramatic effect, "complete me."[7] This movie, already nearly thirty years old, highlights what most every Hollywood romance does—that, whether a marriage or not, any good partnership lives on through the euphoria of romance. The notion that a romantic partner fulfills the deepest parts of our soul is the heartbeat of many reality television shows and romantic comedies.

Scholars who study marriage have noted the heightened emphasis in contemporary relationships on the pursuit of intimacy

---

7. Crowe, *Jerry Maguire*.

and the desire to have our emotional needs met by a partner. Contrasted to early forms of marriage, this model of matrimony is more individualistic and concerned with self-actualization and an internal sense of fulfillment. In many ways, this approach to marriage has increased the expectations individuals place on partners as they enter marriage. Sociologists call this the soulmate marriage.[8]

The rise of the soulmate marriage has coincided with a decline in the authority of and trust in social institutions, such as religious communities, that bolster the marriage commitment, or at least have historically promoted marital norms such as permanence.[9] There is less stigma than in the past around exiting a marriage for any reason, and certainly for the reason that the marriage is no longer emotionally satisfying.

One could argue, and many do, that the contemporary focus on intimacy and fulfillment has led to better marriages. What, after all, would marriage be with people who do not rely on each other emotionally? What about a purely pragmatic marriage—one where boxes are checked and commitments upheld without any gloss of romance? If a marriage is one of duty and obligation alone, it would seem fair in this conception to question whether it is a marriage at all. The reality is, however, that any long-term commitment will have ebbs and flows in feeling. And any long-term commitment is held together by more than one factor; emotional commitment is one of them, but not the only one. Soulmate marriage, then, can mean a more fragile commitment. Still, those who support it suggest that we should reevaluate how we define marital success, focusing less on permanency and more on measures of satisfaction and fulfillment.

While emotional fulfillment is certainly an important aspect of marriage, the soulmate model of marriage is unbalanced. It ultimately produces lower-quality relationships because the inevitable fluctuations of emotional fulfillment and sexual attraction within relationships mean less stability.[10] It imposes unrealistic

8. Wilcox and Dew, "Is Love a Flimsy Foundation?"

9. Wilcox and Dew, "Is Love a Flimsy Foundation?," 688.

10. Wilcox and Dew, "Is Love a Flimsy Foundation?"; Wilcox, "For as Long."

demands on partners, especially over the long term. Instead, a more robust marriage rides out periods of rest or boredom, even frustration, entering again into excitement down the road. The soulmate model, by relying too heavily on emotion and by diminishing the rewards of longevity, ultimately fails to value other aspects of marriage that benefit family members and wider society. If we were Hollywood producers pitching marriage as a movie to a big studio, we'd argue that our script isn't a romance but a Tolkien-like adventure. Marriage is an epic journey with ups and downs, with the ultimate focus on the horizon.

The elevation of personal fulfilment as the chief purpose of marriage is risky. This is especially true when the pursuit of personal fulfillment eclipses the commitment to permanence. There seems to be a niche publishing genre featuring authors proclaiming their liberation from marriages that did not meet their emotional expectations. Divorce is presented as the gateway to personal growth. Perhaps this is the case for these authors, but the dissolution of a marriage is no guarantee to happiness forever after.

Soulmate marriage today relies too heavily on what was once only one component of marriage—love. Love, always a part of marriage,[11] has now conquered marriage, to paraphrase the title of Stephanie Coontz's popular history.[12] But this expression of marriage is incomplete and falls short of the best way for human beings to flourish. Can we imagine a different way?

We start by asking why the human species derived a legally and culturally binding commitment called marriage in the first place. In other words, what are the purpose and function of marriage?

---

11. Anthropologist and historian Alan Macfarlane, author of *Marriage and Love in England*, writes: "The idea of a massive transformation from a group-based, brutal, and unfeeling society to the highly individualized and loving modern one is basically a myth" (as cited in Gairdner, *War against the Family*, 63).

12. Coontz, *Marriage, a History*.

I ... DO?

## Marriage as an Institution

You've likely attended a wedding ceremony where the couple have written their own vows—perhaps you've written your own. One wedding planning-advice website suggests couples keep their vows "light and simple," injecting humor into the exchange of oaths. The site even provides examples: "I vow not to carry on watching a Netflix series we started together without you. Or at least pretend it's the first time I've watched it when we watch it again."[13]

Customization in a wedding ceremony reflects the personalities of the individuals. But we should ask why we do the things we do at weddings. If signing official papers is what makes it legal, why have a ceremony? Why exchange vows and rings? There are many "traditional" aspects of a wedding we do in fact maintain. These actually serve a purpose. They hint at a different understanding of marriage, signaling that individuals are entering an institution. A wedding ceremony is more than an opportunity for personal expression.

In the soulmate model of marriage, the wedding is a validation of one's love and desire to remain together. It is a platform for self-expression, conforming the elements to fit our personalities. But it remains a public expression. In whatever form those vows take, they are typically not written for an audience of two. ("I love your stupid face and vow that I will put up with whatever you can throw at me—if you think you can put up with my mess" is another suggested vow.[14]) We're inviting those in attendance to join us and all our personal quirks in the celebration of love.

The opposing view to the soulmate model of marriage is an institutional view. So what do we mean when we say that marriage is an institution? Institutions are a bundle of formal and informal rules, social norms, legal and natural rights, and obligations.[15] When individuals enter institutions, they voluntarily constrain certain behaviors in order to achieve a particular set of goods or

---

13. Brandwein, "Forty-Five Funny Wedding Vows," no. 11.
14. Brandwein, "Forty-Five Funny Wedding Vows," no. 36.
15. Barzel and Allen, *Economic Analysis*, 137.

outcomes. Institutions are created and evolve to meet needs outside the control of any one individual. Thus the common wedding refrain about couples entering *into* the bonds of matrimony.

Societies create institutions to mitigate the consequence of problems. For institutions to work, communities need to believe these bundles of rules and norms are legitimate and trustworthy, and that they mitigate the problems they were created to address. For this reason, institutions evolve through trial and error.[16] Importantly, institutions are created and evolve outside the control of any one individual.[17] Entering into an institution is not merely a private act. Individuals who enter the institution of marriage choose to alter or constrain behavior to produce a desired outcome. While these constraints may restrict individuals, they produce goods for both the couples and their community.

Imagine a society where parentage is uncertain. What ensures that men provide for the children they father? How do they know which children they fathered? How can mothers ensure that their sexual partners provide for them during pregnancy and beyond? How do societies ensure children are not neglected or abandoned? The evolution of marriage is to some degree a societal response to the uncontrollable nature of fertility. The need for an institution like marriage arose from challenges that Mother Nature threw at societies.

We have more (though not perfect) control over fertility today, and marriage has evolved in response, but it still serves an institutional purpose. University of Virginia sociologist Brad Wilcox puts it this way: "The institutional model of marriage seeks to integrate sex, parenthood, economic cooperation, and emotional intimacy into a permanent union."[18] This model of marriage seeks to bind more elements into permanent unions using voluntary restrictions, sacrifices, or the changing of personal behaviors in exchange for other benefits. It's a more robust framework for marriage, one that, at its best, aims to merge a broad set

---

16. Barzel and Allen, *Economic Analysis*, 141.
17. Barzel and Allen, *Economic Analysis*, 139–40.
18. Wilcox, "When Marriage Disappears," 38.

of social needs for the benefit of individuals, family, and society. There is something surrendered in marriage, but with the belief that what is gained is greater. It's an institution that poses limits on our relationships by its nature. Thus, the soulmate model is at odds with the institutional model of marriage. "You complete me" asks a partner to shore up the gaps in my sense of self. It doesn't typically envision voluntarily constraining oneself for the good of the other, for the good of the partnership, and for the good of the community.

A functioning institution can handle moderations. But we ask you to consider the extent to which marriage is flexible. Which aspects are immutable? What purpose does it serve? What changes do you think everyone accepts, in contrast with those changes that are contested? Answering these questions allows us to come to a shared consensus on the nature of what marriage is as a groundwork for the rest of family life.

## Marriage Is Intimately Linked to Sex

The idea that marriage is intimately linked to sex may not feel true for many, given that it is no longer the only licit place for sexual activity. However, we cannot discuss marriage as an institution without discussing the way in which it evolved to account for normal outcomes of sex. In post-Christian countries we view the idea with derision. But the reasons for having sex inside marriage were not merely religious; they were also practical. The separation of sexual intimacy from marriage has consequences for us today, just as it did in the past.

Asserting that marriage and sex should be linked needs explanation. Prior to the advent of paternity tests and in vitro fertilization, marriage was an easy and effective way to regulate human reproduction and to ensure families stayed together for the care of children. If all of this is sounding prehistoric to you, consider that, depending on your age, this was the case not centuries ago but in all likelihood for your grandparents or, perhaps if you are a young millennial, great-grandparents. For an older generation, one reason to get married was to share every aspect of life, and that included sex. We asked Dan, age sixty-eight, why he got married. In his answer he gave some of the usual reasons about wanting to share a life rather than live alone. Yet he also added what today would be considered a highly unusual reason: "I felt very strongly that if I wanted to pursue a sexual relationship, I wanted to be married."

When sex ceased to be constrained to marriage, this precipitated a lack of commitment between couples and changing attitudes toward children. Courtesy of the technological shock of oral contraceptives, children were no longer an expected outcome from sexual intercourse.[19] No longer did men and women need to remain together "till death do us part"—a proxy for the time and long-suffering it takes to raise a child. When sex no longer meant consideration for the need to raise children together, then the lifelong precondition of marriage in order to have children ceased to make sense. Erika Bachiochi, author of *The Rights of Women*, explains one of the outcomes for marriage: "The decoupling of sex from marriage and marriage from childbearing, ushered in by the sexual revolution," she writes, "unraveled a working-class culture of once stable marital bonds that children need and both mothers and fathers once relied upon for their success at home and at work, and in all of life."[20]

"Free love" was the rallying cry of the 1960s at Woodstock and beyond. We now use terms like being "sex positive," as if there were anyone who is truly sex negative. There's a reverse stigma placed today on the idea that there may be positives associated with constraining sex in any way. At the same time, there are those who are asserting and identifying that free love hasn't always been quite so free, quite so loving, or happened without consequences.

---

19. Did a lack of commitment precede oral contraceptives or the reverse? Did oral contraceptives shift sexual norms such that marriage was no longer the place for sex? These are all big questions to consider. See M. Eberstadt, *Adam and Eve*, for an informed look at these and other questions pertaining to sexual ethics, the sexual revolution, and the advent of oral contraceptives.

20. Bachiochi, *Rights of Women*, 13.

I . . . DO?

Volumes have been written on the consequences associated with unconstrained sexual freedom. Few would contest a breakdown of the relationship between the sexes. Apps intended to facilitate dating connections do anything but.[21] Romance and dating are dead, wrote one thirtysomething around Valentine's Day 2024.[22] Younger and younger people are seeing violent porn, which often makes its way into physical encounters, mostly without any clear consent and changing relationships—not for the better.[23] For a culture in which we claim sex is free and accessible, we are having less of it.[24]

This being true, it comes as little surprise that a more vocal opposition to unconstrained sexuality in the formative lives of young adults is emerging. Take Christine Emba's *Rethinking Sex: A Provocation* (2022), Louise Perry's *The Case against the Sexual Revolution* (2022), and Mary Harrington's *Feminism against Progress* (2023). All make the case that unconstrained sexuality is playing a negative role and raising consequences for many. Once again, it would seem there is no such thing as a free lunch. Rather, there are trade-offs to the various choices we make.

Do these women advise we must return sex to marriage? No, they don't, though one of them comes close. Louise Perry advises in her book for women to wait six months in a relationship before having sex. But two years after publication, Perry, speaking on a podcast, said she wishes she'd been more conservative about that point:

> I made the recommendation in the book for women reading, in particular, to wait for maybe six months into a new relationship before having sex as a way of, you know, having a chance to assess this guy's character,

---

21. Many have made this point, but endless swiping without connection to one's social network results in no social pressure to behave well while forming relationships.

22. Trinko, "Dating Crisis Fuels Marriage Crisis."

23. Van Maren, "How Porn Is Ruining."

24. Much has been written on the "sex recession," which may be linked to a decline in marriage, where people have more sex (Willingham, "Having Less Sex").

not be befuddled by hormones, all that stuff. And I did think at the time, should I just go for it and say wait until engagement or wait until marriage? Because what better indication is there of genuine commitment? . . . And my mom said, no, don't, because if you say that, that's the only thing anyone will remember about that book. And that will be the first line of every review, you know, crazy lady makes the case for waiting until marriage. . . . I also think actually probably waiting till engagement is what I would tell my children to do. So maybe I should have said that.[25]

There are many different ways to be labeled as crazy. But what could certainly warrant the adjective is a worldview in which sex is the equivalent of a hobby or a sports activity rather than one that plays an intrinsic part in a lasting relationship. Marriage, as it turns out, does more than allow for paternity to be known in sexual relations for purposes of the care of children and transfer of property. Constraining sex to marriage also places guardrails around this important aspect of human behavior that is so easily abused, even when a child is not the result.

The whole push for consent in sexual activity is a quiet acknowledgment of the need for guardrails. The lowest bar is consent—and it's a critically important one. But there are always legal boundaries and norms we all must follow, or people get hurt. Witness the #MeToo movement as one example of the many ways in which hurts ensue out of nebulous sexual contacts. Ultimately, everyone can indeed have sex outside marriage, but many at this point may be longing for the voluntary constraints marriage furnishes, pointing relationships toward longevity and stability.

Unconstrained sexual freedom can also look like it works for educated, upper-income-level people. Well-heeled folks have money to buffer bad decisions. But the lack of marriage has been a disaster for lower-income echelons. Rob Henderson expands on this at length in his book *Troubled*. Henderson coined the term *luxury beliefs*, which are beliefs that the wealthy can afford to hold

---

25. Perry, "Modern Dating Catastrophe," 2:21.

but of which the poor suffer the consequences. Even so, the upper classes tend to talk left but walk right, meaning that even as they advance progressive notions in theory, they are more likely to get married and have children within marriage.

Increasingly, feminists are noting that the sexual revolution broke down marriage but in so doing offered nothing in its stead. Biological realities that cannot be eradicated make sex a consequential act, one that is more happily engaged in with boundaries around it precisely because, even in an age of modern birth control, conception after sex cannot be ruled out.

Today, unconstrained sexuality means relationships often start with sex. This can cloud judgment, which may mean making a poor choice in a marriage partner.[26] While data do not show that premarital sex leads to the poor choice of a marriage partner, we do know that multiple premarital sexual partners is a predictor for divorce.[27] Our culture suggests it's important to start relationships in bed rather than, say, with budgeting, but this reflects the rise of sexual revolution values and the diminished marriage culture we now share. For too many it doesn't matter whether the sexual contact lasts, and it is likewise easy to believe that sex is the start of emotional bonding rather than the culmination of it. C. S. Lewis once called sex outside marriage a "monstrosity" (something unnatural or misshapen). He did not do so because it doesn't follow Christian theology or rules, but because those who engage in sex outside marriage "are trying to isolate one kind of union (the sexual) from all the other kinds of union which were intended to go along with it and make up the total union."[28]

Sex and marriage are as intertwined as love and marriage, even when we no longer view them that way.

---

26. Santos-Longhurst, "Love Hormone."
27. Smith and Wolfinger, "Re-Examining the Link."
28. Lewis, *Joyful Christian*, 199.

## Marriage as the Foundation for Family Life

Marriage commits parents to each other and those parents to their children. Views of marriage as subjugating women now dominate our approach not just to family life but also to family policy. But marriage places constraints on men as well as women: it is a way of guaranteeing a man's involvement in family.

There has never been a successful society where fathers did not support mothers by obligation. James Q. Wilson, author of *The Marriage Problem*, writes, "There is no society where women alone care for each other and their children; there is none where fathers are not obligated to support their children and the mothers to whom they were born."[29] Part of the reason for marriage over the millennia has been to establish clear family lines and to know which men are responsible for which children. (It's always been more obvious via nine months of pregnancy which woman was responsible.) Marriage ensured we knew and understood where we came from, alongside the mainstays of economic wealth and wealth transfer. When people married, they married into a family, and family had a say in whom they married.

Marriage exposes women's need for men—or, better put, mothers' needs for fathers. For women, marriage and having children are intimately related. Marriage brings men into the child-rearing proposition not by using women as a tool but rather by helping them. After all, "a mother alone," writes David Blankenhorn, author of *The Future of Marriage*,

> is not enough for the slowly maturing human child. She needs someone to help provide food. She and the child need protection from predators and other dangers. She needs someone to relieve, spell, and comfort her. She needs a companion that she can count on. She needs someone to be her partner in raising the child—someone who will love the child (almost) as much as she does and who is willing to sacrifice deeply and permanently for the child's sake. In short, to increase the likelihood

---

29. Wilson, *Marriage Problem*, 29.

of survival and success, the human infant needs a father and the human mother needs a mate.[30]

Children need their fathers, true. But even as we talk about men supporting children by obligation, we can acknowledge that men need children. Evidence suggests men benefit and grow from participation in family life. Not only do many men find great meaning in being fathers, but there is evidence that it influences their biology. Fathers, and particularly those who spend more time with children, have been found to experience a reduction in testosterone. Why may this be a positive development? The reduction in testosterone may reduce levels of male aggression. Richard Reeves, formerly of the Brookings Institution and now president of the American Institute for Boys and Men, suggests that the increases in the portion of married men raising families collectively reduces levels of male violence. He reports that scholars studying this natural repression of testosterone production point out that "human males have an evolved neuroendocrine architecture shaped to facilitate their role as fathers and caregivers as a key component of reproductive success."[31] So the prevalence of fathers in a community may reduce male aggression, and this reduction may make men better suited to caregiving.

If we understand from the start that marriage protects lines of connection to children, we begin to realize there is an important attitude embedded in marriage, which is that it is oriented to the future. Institutional marriage is child centered, whereas soulmate marriage sees romantic relationship as an end in itself. There is a greater emphasis in the relationship on the two adults themselves, without the emphasis on procreative capacity.

## Marriage as the Path to Creating Community

It has become cliché, in certain circles at least, to say that family is the building block of community and society. Family is the little

---

30. Blankenhorn, *Future of Marriage*, 35.
31. As quoted in Reeves, *Of Boys and Men*, 95.

platoon, the first society. A vibrant economy or flourishing society requires healthy families. But what does this actually mean?

Family is the sine qua non of learning to live in community. We all start out within our families, and from there, we branch out to learn how to live with others—extended family, daycares, schools. Wherever we end up going as small children, we begin in family—it's where we learn to navigate differences, to support and help one another, and, importantly, it's where we learn to love. Developmental psychologist Gordon Neufeld writes of a child's capacity for healthy relationship "unfolding" in the first six years of life.[32] Family is the primary place where children learn and are formed as people. We don't often stop to ponder this point, but a stable and healthy home life contributes to a healthy citizenry.

Marriage continues to be relevant today, in part because it is future focused on life beyond ourselves. This need not come exclusively through having children of one's own. The longevity and stability of marriage are themselves social goods. Sometimes this kind of good becomes more notable through its absence. When some of my (Andrea's) good friends divorced, it became clear that the connection with both sides of the couple—both previously cherished people in my life—would become difficult if not impossible. In a way, the couple had been an entity all on its own and a way of connecting into the life of that family.

The post-World War II married-parent, "nuclear" family has been criticized for being a closed enclave isolated in the suburbs. Some aspects of the critique are well founded: based on our culture's prioritization of independence and autonomy, we have the idea that we can do family life all on our own without extended family. Certainly, this isn't the vision of family life we are after. But the argument too often conflates the problem of isolated families in the postwar era with the idea that the intact, married-parent family is somehow responsible for this isolation. In fact, the trend of family isolation and transience is something we experience in many of our relationships, not just marriage.

---

32. Neufeld and Maté, *Hold On to Your Kids*.

Recently, the idea of friendship as a central organizing force for society has gained in popularity. Take for example Rhaina Cohen's book *The Other Significant Others: Reimagining Life with Friendship at the Center*. Cohen raises a good question: Could friendship, not marriage, be at the center of our lives? Could friendship achieve the same level of social stability as marriage?

We are skeptical that the answer to these questions is yes. Friendships more closely approximate cohabiting relationships. And the evidence on cohabiting relationships is that they are less stable than marriage for varying reasons. Marriage is the gold standard for parents sticking together for raising children. Deep, lasting, and unique friendships are a wonderful way to provide companionship and solidarity in any number of different circumstances, including but not limited to family breakdown. A single mother, for example, has a more pressing need for stable friendships in her life and will rightly seek them out, finding them to replace the presence of a father in the home. That this is a social good is true. That friendships such as these act as a one-to-one replacement for marriage is not.

We know other aspects of marriage also contribute to community. Many families, especially intact, married-parent families, interact through community clubs, organizations, and places of worship. Marriage is linked to increased social networks and rates of volunteerism. While community involvement can ebb and flow throughout the course of family life, marriage is generally associated with greater community involvement.[33] Many families are hospitable, caring environments for extended family and friends and do not fit the stereotype of the isolated nuclear family at all. As our population ages, these caregiving units will become increasingly important in the life of neighborhoods and communities. In any event, what we are advocating for are stable marriages at the heart of extended family and reaching into community, not isolated nuclear families.

---

33. Stuart, "How Family Status."

# 2

# The Marriage Advantage

AT THANKSGIVING, JOURNALISTS OFTEN ask pedestrians on the street the standard question "What are you thankful for?" "My family" is among the most common responses. Family is central in our lives. Because family is an important part of our personal lives, we tend not to talk about family structure and its link to social issues. It feels awkward and at worst judgmental to weigh in on family formation, especially in social settings. Yet what feels awkward to discuss in personal settings, such as around the dinner table, is equally problematic to avoid in academic and public policy discussions.

The weight of existing research points to the centrality of family formation for our well-being in community, in health, in children's outcomes, in wealth, and in general well-being. And while family dissolution or trauma is often outside personal control, greater knowledge of the benefits of marriage and family among thought leaders, teachers, academics, and others may be one way to achieve a marriage-friendly culture and help young people to achieve relational stability in their own lives. Public discussion should address the centrality of good marriages for the good life.

This section offers relevant research showing positive attributes of marriage. We do a disservice when we ignore decades of social science research on the impact of family structure, related as it is to family stability in policy discussions.

How much evidence shows that married people tend to accumulate more wealth, enjoy better health and fulfillment, and their children experience better outcomes on a number of measures? At this point, quite a bit. These benefits have been termed *the marriage advantage* in the social sciences. We've already said, but it's worth repeating, we are inviting you to look beyond your own experience, positive or negative, and consider how a robust marriage culture and the benefits of this way of living have bearing on our shared lives in our communities. Without detracting from the challenges arising in unhealthy or abusive marriages, we want to first imagine the possibility that there is a good news story associated with healthy marriage.

The key caveat when discussing the benefits of marriage is that the advantages are correlated with *healthy* marriages. High-conflict, low-quality marriages are correlated with the opposite—poorer well-being. Samantha, a Gen-Xer we asked for her views on marriage, says this: "I think that most psychiatric issues in the walking wounded boil down to questions of love, security, and agency. Marriage is ideally a place where the raw needs of unconditional love and safety/support can be most readily met. Agency is where the rub occurs, perhaps. Were marriage to be again foundational, rates of mental illness, substance abuse, identity confusion, and even simple erosion of esteem would all be ameliorated."

There are, broadly, two hypotheses that explain the marriage advantage. The first is the selection effect hypothesis, which means that people with certain characteristics self-select into marriage. Individuals with more education, those who are happier to start with, or those who exhibit other characteristics of well-being are more likely to marry, accounting for a greater portion of married people having these attributes.

The second explanation is the marriage protection hypothesis. This theory posits that marriage moderates behaviors, such as reducing risky behavior and increasing productivity among men. It also posits that marriage provides social supports, including social networks, that increase well-being. Getting married, in other words, provides the necessary support to achieve better well-being. There is evidence for both hypotheses, and the degree that selection or protection contribute to well-being likely depends on the outcome being examined.

Marriage is not a panacea for social problems, nor is it a prerequisite for a fulfilling life. Yet marriage correlates with many benefits for adults and children that contribute to the common good. We cannot ignore decades of data in our public discussions on well-being.

### The Marriage Advantage for Men

Shortly before I (Peter Jon) got married, my friends planned a surprise evening out as a rather mild bachelor party. I was "kidnapped" and compelled to wear a prisoner's uniform accompanied with a fifteen-pound ball and chain secured to my ankle. The implication, of course, was that I was about to lose my freedom, chained down and imprisoned.

The irony lost on my friends at the time was that married men are less likely to participate in the types of deviant behavior that would land one in actual prison. Marriage is good for men. In fact, married men are generally happier, earn more money, and have better economic outcomes than their unmarried peers. They are also less likely to engage in risky or harmful behaviors such as substance abuse. Here, we focus on how marriage shapes men.

Marriage is the institution that bonds men to their partners and their children. Men are historically unreliable in reporting their fertility involvement to pollsters, either unaware of the totality of their fertility history or failing to acknowledge children with whom they do not live. Sociologist David Popenoe notes that the "legitimacy" of children has been a near universal concern across societies. He argues that men do not have the biological imperative to be committed fathers in the way that women do to be mothers. That may sound antiquated to the modern, committed father, but the truth is that the relationship between mother and father is critical to father involvement. Popenoe concludes, "The decline of marriage is a disaster for fatherhood. . . . Men tend to view marriage and childbearing as a single package. If their marriage deteriorates, their fathering deteriorates."[1]

The relationship between mothers and fathers influences how men who don't live with their children raise their kids. The success of contemporary fatherhood initiatives that focus on increasing bonds between nonresidential fathers and their children often hinge on mothers who act as gatekeepers to the children.[2] These programs may improve father-child interactions, but they have been shown to be less successful in increasing the quantity of time nonresidential fathers spend with their children. Certainly, many nonresidential fathers are desperate to spend more time with their children, but again, this illustrates how the mother-father relationship mediates fatherhood.

A general manager for a professional hockey team once quipped to a journalist that he anticipated an up-and-coming player to show greater consistency on the ice because the rising star had gotten married during the offseason. The general manager's hockey sense detected something economists have shown empirically: that married men tend to be more productive at work, as observed through increased work hours and increased earned pay.[3]

In older parlance, rather than saying marriage shapes men, we might say that it civilizes men. That's not to say that single men are unproductive barbarians, but to acknowledge that large populations of unattached and often idle young men have been an issue for societies across history. As Popenoe notes, few institutions outside the military and organized religion form men the way marriage does.[4]

This is not to say that it is the duty of women to reform men through marriage. This would be no partnership. Rather, marriage

1. Popenoe, *Life without Father*, 25.
2. Kearney, *Two-Parent Privilege*, 144.
3. Wilcox and Wolfinger, *Men and Marriage*, 2.
4. Popenoe, *Life without Father*, 76.

often focuses men as they engage new priorities as husbands and fathers.

While marriage rates have declined, boys and men have been increasingly struggling in school, work, and family life. Men seem to be falling behind on many social measures. Author and social psychologist Jonathan Haidt has observed that, over decades, boys have been checking out, withdrawing from important social institutions that form and shape us.[5] The withdrawal from family life is particularly evident when observing marriage. While marriage rates have declined for decades, they have fallen more dramatically among those with less education, creating a marriage gap observable along socioeconomic lines.[6] Those with postsecondary education are more likely to marry and stay married, compared with their less educated peers. Those without postsecondary degrees are more likely to be unpartnered or to live in cohabiting relationships that tend to be more fragile than marriage. The marriage gap means that men and women who would benefit most from stable partnerships are missing out on the advantages associated with marriage.

Some observers have suggested that educational attainment is the key. With better access to educational opportunities, men could more easily connect with meaningful employment, increasing their economic standing and potential for entry into family life. The relationship between these factors, however, is more complex. American political economist Nicholas Eberstadt has studied the decline of work among prime-aged men—in particular, the increasing portion of unattached prime-aged men not in the labor force and not looking for work. He notes that this long-term decline coincides with the long-term fall of the married two-parent family structure. Educational attainment is a significant factor, and married men tend to have higher levels of educational attainment. Eberstadt notes, however, that married men with low levels of educational attainment are more attached to the labor force than slightly higher educated but never married

5. Haidt, "Why I'm Increasingly Worried."
6. Wilcox and Wang, "Marriage Divide."

men. He also states that there are notable differences in labor force participation between married and unmarried men with similar skill levels.[7] He concludes that poor economic opportunities among less educated men may inhibit family formation, but it doesn't account for the whole story. Family structure plays a role and should be further studied.

The function of marriage in stable family life is often neglected in conversations about the crisis of retreating men. Family structure is one of the most important factors in low-income children's ability to enter the middle class as adults.[8] It is also true that the link between marriage and income is rarely expressed to young adults.

The able-bodied, prime-aged man not in the labor force that Eberstadt worries about is also a less attractive mate. As sociologist Brad Wilcox demonstrates from survey data, modern women still value productive and protective-minded mates. Additionally, they want a partner who will be attentive to their emotional needs. Wilcox describes these relationships as neo-traditional marriages.[9] Yet the able-bodied, prime-aged men not in the labor force don't exhibit the characteristics women find attractive. This reduces their potential for marriage and shrinks the pool of potential suitable mates for many women.

I (Peter Jon) sheepishly admit to occasionally watching matchmaking and reality dating shows with my better half—for research purposes, of course. On a recent reality TV romance show, a young couple were considering the prospect of marriage. The would-be future husband asked his partner whether men received a ring during the wedding ceremony, or just the bride. This may seem like a silly question, but viewers learn during the episode that the young man had never known a married man while he was growing up. In his community, marriage was absent, and the common act of wearing a wedding ring was unfamiliar to him. In his

---

7. N. Eberstadt, "Family Structure and Decline," 136–39.
8. Wilcox and Bullivant, "American Dream Can Be Achieved."
9. Wilcox, *Get Married*, 172.

experience, not only did men not marry, but few men remained faithful to their partners.

Marriage is an institution that requires community support. Healthy marriage relationships need to be modeled in order to be replicated. In the absence of men modeling healthy partnerships to other men, the decline of marriage becomes a self-fulfilling prophecy in a weakening marriage culture.

As we have noted, marriage isn't for everyone. Yet there is merit in educating young adults about marriage so they can decide for themselves. The evidence shows that young adults who complete their education, marry, and then have children, in that order, can significantly reduce the chances of experiencing poverty.[10] The *success sequence*, as it is called, doesn't avoid all the systemic barriers young adults face, but it does provide a pathway to avoid poverty and an opportunity to educate about the role of marriage in stable family life.

## The Marriage Advantage for Women

Marriage is good for women. Given the volume of literature written in recent decades making the opposite case, it's fair to wonder how this is even possible. For decades, even centuries, feminists have made the case that marriage is a form of slavery, an institution that keeps women under men's thumbs and treats them like chattel. But is this true?

Of late, a new generation of feminists is naming marriage as not just a social good but a good for women, specifically mothers. That marriage is a social good is as true for women as it is for men, though the case may be slightly more complicated to make.

At least one of the problems with being against marriage for women is that those same voices are not uniformly against women having sexual relationships with men, which have something of a probability of resulting in children. And thus far in human society, there is virtually no solution so helpful on the horizon as

---

10. W. Wang and Wilcox, *Power of Success Sequence*.

marriage to help women who become mothers. Because sex is still consequential, Louise Perry says, and because the results of sexual activity do not have the same outcomes for women as for men (a form of "sexual asymmetry"[11]), women even today in a world with few stigmas around extramarital sexual activity can find themselves in traumatic situations when the father does not stick around. Lone-parent poverty is almost entirely made up of single mothers (not to diminish the difficulty the rising numbers of lone fathers experience, but this is still statistically true). And lone-mother poverty is something to which our current policy-makers have dedicated time and attention attempting to fix. Yet even where finances could be sorted—in Canada, cash benefits for parents geared to income seem to have reduced the rate of child poverty—the children of lone parents still face the same obstacles any child outside the two-parent privilege faces.[12]

Women who become mothers need care and protection themselves in order to care for and protect their babies. The fathers of those children make very good candidates to take on this role. And there is much reason and research supporting the notion that marriage is not incidental to fathers sticking around. Yes, fathers are valuable, necessary, and nonnegotiable to their children whether they are married to the mothers or not. But fathers are more likely to stick around to care for their kids when married to the mother of those same children.

There is also evidence that married women are indeed happy—and happier than their unmarried peers. American survey data from 2022 show higher happiness rates for married women, with or without children. The "biggest happiness dividends" for women, write Wilcox and Wang, are found in a combination of marriage and parenthood.[13] The women most likely to say they are "not too happy" are unmarried women without children.[14]

11. "Sexual asymmetry" is a term Bachiochi uses in her book *Rights of Women*.

12. Kearney, *Two-Parent Privilege*.

13. Wilcox and Wang, "Who Is Happiest?," para. 2.

14. Marina Adshade acknowledges the happiness dividend of marriage while providing context and caveats ("Does Marriage").

Young women today have a vast range of options for career, service, and work. Prioritizing these options, however, can overshadow getting married and starting a family, and this can create a conundrum when women grow older without any change in family status. Canadian and American surveys tell the story of women at the end of their reproductive lives wishing for more children than they have.[15]

Contrary to the point of view that marriage works to the benefit of men but enslaves women, marriage particularly constrains men in ways that are more conducive to a happy, healthy, and wealthy life for women.

### The Marriage Advantage for Fertility: An Advantage for Women and Men

As the evidence shows, marriage is a child-centered institution. Of course, having children doesn't legitimize any one couple's marriage over another's, but a healthy marriage does benefit kids, and marriage means the ability to have the children women say they want. Canadian survey data show one reason women who want children aren't having them is the lack of suitable partners.[16]

Canada recorded a historic low total fertility rate (TFR) of 1.33 births per woman in 2022. A population requires a TFR of 2.1 to replace itself from generation to generation.[17] The TFR in the United States was only slightly better in 2022, at 1.66. Fertility across North America is now so low that politicians, policymakers, and public commentators are compelled to address the issue.

Many economic and cultural factors have contributed to declining fertility in Western countries and across the globe, and the decline of marriage is one contributing issue. Most births in

---

15. Canada: Stone, "She's (Not) Having a Baby"; USA: Stone, "How Many Kids."

16. Only women were surveyed (Stone, "She's [Not] Having a Baby").

17. The TFR is an estimate of the number of children that a hypothetical woman will have over her lifetime, based on age-specific fertility rates within a given year. Canada has not recorded a replacement level TFR of 2.1 since 1971.

Canada and the United States are to married women, but adults in both countries are marrying less and at later ages, compared with several decades ago. The increase in the age at first birth results in a shorter period to have the number of children couples desire. In many countries there is a gap between the actual fertility rate and desired fertility. While many believe low fertility represents increased female empowerment, there is substantial evidence in North America that our low fertility rates represent, in part, unfulfilled life goals.

Furthermore, US data show that the overwhelming majority of abortions occur among unmarried women. "The vast majority of women who had abortions in 2021 were unmarried (87 percent), while married women accounted for 13 percent, according to the CDC, which had data on this from 37 states," Pew Research tell us.[18] While data on abortion by marital status is not readily available in Canada, over half of all abortions happen among women younger than the average age of first marriage. Without diving into the thorny issue of abortion, it's still worth noting that over eight in ten abortions in the United States happen among women who are not married. If we accept that abortion is a difficult thing for any woman to undergo, we can then imagine that married couples are more likely to have the economic means and social and family support to navigate unplanned pregnancy, compared with the level of support among many unmarried women facing similar circumstances. Surveys show that women want to have more children than they are currently having, but under the right circumstances—marriage being a key factor.

Multiple factors contribute to the global decline in fertility rates; however, marriage and fertility remain firmly linked.[19] Absent a marriage-friendly culture, fertility rates will not increase and women will not have the number of children they desire.

---

18. Diamant et al., "Abortion in the US," under subheading "What Are the Demographics of Women Who Have Had Abortions?"

19. Stone and James, *Marriage Still Matters*.

## The Marriage Advantage for Children

Decades of research shows that the married-parent family is the gold standard for child-rearing. The respected research organization Child Trends concludes, "Research clearly demonstrates that family structure matters for children, and the family structure that helps children the most is a family headed by two biological parents in a low-conflict marriage."[20]

Children from married-parent homes tend to have better educational outcomes. They are more likely to be read to at home, less likely to miss class, and more likely to graduate high school.[21] Children from married-, biological-parent families are more likely to attain higher levels of education, compared with their peers from other family structures.[22]

Emotional and behavioral outcomes likewise tend to be better among children from married-parent homes. Children in married-, biological-parent homes have lower levels of behavioral and emotional problems, compared with peers from other family structures.[23] Studies have found that children from two-parent homes are less likely to attempt suicide, experience mental illness, or abuse drugs.[24]

Further, children with married parents are less likely to experience poverty. A US Census-based study found that children with married parents are three times less likely to live in poverty, compared with children in lone-parent, cohabiting-mother, or unmarried-, biological-parent families.[25]

Wilcox has found that children from intact, married-parent homes were much more likely to attain a college degree,

---

20. Moore et al., *Marriage from Child's Perspective*, 6.
21. Witherspoon Institute, *Marriage and Public Good*, 9.
22. Wu et al., "Family Structure and University Enrollment."
23. Brown, "Family Structure and Child Well-Being."
24. Witherspoon Institute, *Marriage and Public Good*, 10.
25. Kreider, "Living Arrangements of Children."

enhancing future employment prospects. This was particularly true for children in less privileged families.[26]

Canadian economist Frank Jones examined data from Statistics Canada's National Longitudinal Survey of Children and Youth and found that teens who had unmarried, cohabiting parents as children were more likely to engage in risk behaviors and have poorer relationships with their parents, compared with their peers whose parents were married when they were children.[27]

Marriage binds a child's biological parents together. Sociologists Sara McLanahan and Gary Sandefur have argued,

> If we were asked to design a system for making sure that children's basic needs were met, we would probably come up with something quite similar to the two-parent ideal. Such a design, in theory, would not only ensure that children had access to the time and money of two adults, it also would provide a system of checks and balances that promoted quality parenting. The fact that both parents have a *biological* connection to the child would increase the likelihood that the parents would identify with the child and be willing to sacrifice for that child, and it would reduce the likelihood that either parent would abuse the child.[28]

And while McLanahan and Sandefur use the term "two-parent ideal," not "marriage," in the quote above, marriage in other research proves itself as the way two parents are most likely to stay together over the long haul. A study of families in the United Kingdom found that 75 percent of couples who were already married at the birth of their child remained together fifteen years later, compared with 31 percent of cohabiting parents who never married.[29] Healthy, stable home environments are good for kids, and marriage increases the probability of growing up in a stable family.

26. Wilcox, "Marriage Makes Our Children Richer."

27. Mitchell, *Growing Up Married*.

28. Witherspoon Institute, *Marriage and Public Good*, 12 (emphasis original).

29. Benson, "Act of Marriage," para. 5.

Reviewing a decade of literature, sociologist Susan Brown argues that neither stability nor marriage alone are "sufficient to maximize child outcomes."[30] She points to differences, on average, in outcomes between children in intact married parent and married stepfamilies, and differences in outcomes between intact married families and intact cohabiting families. Neither stability nor marriage alone confers the level of advantage, on average, of a stable, married-parent home.

## The Marriage Advantage for Couples

### Happiness

A small kerfuffle erupted among academics in 2019 when London School of Economics economist Paul Dolan provided the *Guardian* newspaper a doozy of a quote in promoting his book on happiness. Dolan told the paper that according to his research "married people are happier than other population subgroups, but only when their spouse is in the room when they're asked how happy they are. When the spouse is not present: f***ing miserable." In short, married people are secretly unhappy. This quote received broad exposure. Here, finally, was proof that marriage is not only unnecessary but also makes you miserable. His conclusion was based on data from the American Time Use Survey, in which participants journaled about their happiness and were required to note if someone else was in the room while they completed their entry. Dolan's quip departs from decades of research, and as it turns out, he ended up retracting it; he was actually making unsupported assumptions about marital happiness and the nature of the relationship between the respondent and the other person who was in the room during the journal entry.[31] The quote has since been stricken from the article.

Looking at available research on happiness and marital status in Canada and the United States, the data over the last fifty years

---

30. Brown, "Marriage and Child Well-Being," 1065.
31. Wolfinger, "Are Married People Still Happier?"

suggests married people are indeed happier than those who have never married.[32] International studies show that married couples are happier, compared with cohabiting couples.[33] Some evidence suggests the marriage-happiness correlation is an artifact of selection effect, mentioned above. Happier people are more likely to attract a spouse and get married. Certainly, selection effect may be a factor, but it doesn't tell the whole story. In this case, data also show that happiness increases among married couples over time.[34]

## Health

We've all heard a story of a reluctant husband being prompted by his wife to see a doctor, only to be diagnosed with a condition that would otherwise become more severe if left untreated. Perhaps the story is cliché, but loved ones do look out for each other and provide appropriate nudges toward preventative health.

Noted sociologist Linda Waite concluded twenty years ago, "The evidence from four decades of research is surprisingly clear: a good marriage is both men's and women's best bet for living a long, healthy life."[35] These benefits extend beyond keeping tabs on one another. Numerous studies indicate that married people tend to have

- Lower risk of suffering a heart attack
- Better odds of surviving a heart attack
- Quicker recovery from illness
- Higher likelihood of recovering from cancer
- Healthier habits and lifestyles
- Better responses to psychological stress[36]

32. Stone, "Does Getting Married."
33. Stack and Eshleman, "Marital Status and Happiness."
34. Stone, "Does Getting Married."
35. Waite and Gallagher, *Case for Marriage*, 64.
36. Martinuk, "Good for Your Health."

Again, it is *healthy* marriage that is correlated with better health. High-conflict, low-quality marriages contribute to poor health, such as increased blood pressure, risk of heart disease, and poor mental health.[37]

Consider further evidence connecting marriage and health. Numerous studies find being married correlates with better survival rates from cancer.[38] One study of 735,000 patients found that married people lived 20 percent longer than those who were widowed, divorced, or separated. When controlling for lifestyle factors, survival rates were still higher among married patients. Researchers suspect that the personal support provided through marriage contributes to better disease detection, treatment, and ultimately survival.[39] A meta-analysis of eighty-seven studies found that being married was associated with a 12 percent decrease in the risk of dying among cancer patients. The risk was higher for never-married patients, compared with widowed, divorced, or separated patients.[40]

A few years ago, the Heart Institute at the University of Ottawa piloted a program called Healing Hearts Together, aimed at couples with a partner experiencing a cardiac event or procedure. The aim of the relationship program was to "enhance couples' relationship quality, and mental and physical health."[41] The researchers were informed by previous data showing, for instance, that bypass surgery patients were three times as likely to be alive fifteen years after the procedure, compared with those without such support. Participants in Healing Hearts Together reported "positive changes in relationship quality, anxiety, depression, and quality of life."[42] This pilot project is consistent with data showing

37. Martinuk, "Good for Your Health."

38. University of Maryland Medical Center, "Married Lung Cancer Patients"; Nichols, "Marital Status Is Independent Predictor"; Krongrad et al., "Marriage and Mortality"; L. Wang et al., "Marital Status and Colon Cancer."

39. Aizer et al., "Marital Status and Survival."

40. Pinquart and Duberstein, "Associations of Social Networks."

41. University of Ottawa Heart Institute, "Healing Hearts Together," para. 1.

42. University of Ottawa Heart Institute, "Healing Hearts Together," program overview, para. 4.

that married people have better survival rates after heart attacks and cardiac surgery.[43]

A systematic review and meta-analysis of thirty-four studies with a combined over two million participants spanning fifteen countries examined the relationship between marital status and cardiovascular disease, coronary disease, and stroke. The study found elevated risk of dying from coronary heart disease and stroke among unmarried participants, compared with married participants. There was an increased risk of death from coronary heart disease and stroke among divorced participants, but no elevated risk among those who were widowed.[44]

Another study found that married people are at lower risk of having a cardiac event, whereas unmarried men and women have higher odds of mortality from a cardiac event, even when age is taken into consideration.[45] These findings show the importance of supportive relationships, like marriage, both in preventative health and physical and emotional recovery.

Healthy marriage and the support drawn from a good partnership contribute to positive mental health. A study in the *Journal of Health and Social Behavior* found that "one of the most consistent findings in psychiatric epidemiology is that married persons enjoy better health than the unmarried. Researchers have consistently found the highest rates of mental disorder among the divorced and separated, the lowest rates among the married and intermediate rates for the single and widowed."[46] The marriage advantage is evident when reviewing data on depression, psychological well-being, and suicidal ideation, compared with the unmarried, widowed, divorced, and separated.[47] A meta-analysis of sixty-six

---

43. Alviar et al., "Association of Marital Status"; Lammintausta et al., "Acute Coronary Events"; Neuman and Werner, "Postoperative Functional Recovery"; King and Reis, "Marriage and Long-Term Survival."

44. Wong et al., "Risk of Cardiovascular Diseases."

45. Lammintausta et al., "Acute Coronary Events."

46. Williams et al., "Psychiatric Disorders," 141.

47. Stack and Eshleman, "Marital Status and Happiness"; Hughes and Waite, "Marital Biography and Health"; Amato, "Marriage, Cohabitation,

cross-sectional and twenty-seven longitudinal studies examined the relationship between marital quality and personal well-being as measured by depressive symptoms, self-esteem, life satisfaction, physical health, and happiness. The analysis concluded that higher marital quality was associated with better well-being.[48]

## Financial Well-Being

Marriage is associated with numerous economic advantages. For example, economic behavior among married couples differs from those in cohabiting relationships. Married couples are more likely to pool income and leverage money and are more likely to invest in retirement saving and other long-term investments, while cohabiters tend to focus on nonfinancial assets such as vehicles and household items.[49] A 2018 study determined that married couples who never cohabited had the highest net worth, compared with other pairings.[50]

Studies have found that married men tend to work longer hours, are less likely to be fired, and are more likely to earn more than their single peers. In fact, research suggests that married men make between 10 and 40 percent more than their unmarried peers.[51] Perhaps men who tend to marry are also more likely to display attributes that lead to earning more money. It is also possible that being a husband and father motivates men to earn more to support their families.

Marriage is linked to income in North America. Higher-income earners are much more likely to be married than their unmarried peers.[52] This divide has grown over time but has drawn

---

Mental Health"; Schoenborn, "Marital Status and Health"; Waite and Gallagher, *Case for Marriage*.

48. Proulx et al., "Marital Quality."

49. Britt-Lutter et al., "Financial Implications of Cohabitation," 44; Hamplova et al., "One Pot or Two Pot," 380.

50. Britt-Lutter et al., "Financial Implications of Cohabitation," 40.

51. Wilcox and Wolfinger, *Men and Marriage*, 2.

52. Wilcox and Wang, "Marriage Divide"; Mitchell and Cross, "Marriage Gap."

little examination when considering public policy conversations around poverty and economic inequality.⁵³

## The Marriage Advantage for Our Shared Lives

Marriage remains the most stable family form, and family stability is good for children and parents. Speaking on Father's Day, President Barack Obama declared, "Of all the rocks upon which we build our lives, we are reminded today that family is the most important."⁵⁴ Why? Because marriage provides social and emotional support that contributes to the well-being of adults and children. It shapes the behavior of its members toward partners and children. While these benefits accrue to individuals and couples, they collectively contribute to greater stability within communities through the economic and physical health benefits marriage brings individuals. There is a community impact to the individual decisions we all make.

Marriage is also integral to sustaining a country's fertility rate needed for economic productivity and to sustain the social safety net. But when families fragment, the burden of support frequently falls on the state to support families and their children. Marriage can also contribute to sustaining natural caregiving communities, and evidence suggests that married people are more likely to volunteer and be active in civic engagement.⁵⁵

President Obama went on to lament the loss of the presence of fathers in many communities, and the impact this loss has had on boys in particular.⁵⁶ A study published in 2019 examining neighborhood-level outcomes found that the presence of Black dads in a community was correlated with greater social mobility

---

53. Milke, "Missing Family Dynamics."
54. Obama, "Fatherhood Speech," para. 5.
55. Kim and Dew, "Religion and Volunteering."
56. Father absence is not solely a marriage matter. However, we would argue that marriage correlates with the increased presence of fathers in their children's lives.

among Black boys, even among those boys who did not have a father at home.[57] No government program, charity, or even great friendship can completely replicate the function of a healthy, stable family.

Acknowledging the marriage advantage does not condemn other family structures nor prevent supportive policies for all families. As we consistently note, not every person need marry, but the point is, or should be, that a critical mass of married families is good for society. In conveying this concept, author Jonah Goldberg equates the function of marriage in culture to the presence of trees in the ecosystem. Trees hold moisture, their roots prevent soil erosion, and they convert carbon dioxide to oxygen. As clear-cutting in the rainforest has shown, removing trees changes the ecosystem, causing ecological changes extending beyond the immediate location.[58] Unfortunately, the contribution of marriage to the common good is most observable in the places it is most in decline. Comparing the presence and absence of intact families at the neighborhood level is revealing.

Marriage has declined far more rapidly among lower-income North Americans and, with it, the economic and social capital advantages associated with marriage. Lower-income and less educated North Americans are less likely to marry and stay married, compared with their more educated and higher-income peers. If there is a community benefit to married families, the very communities that need this the most are facing higher likelihoods of the absence of marriage.

Urbanist Joel Kotkin and colleagues suggest that the collective trend toward declining marriage and fertility reflects a transition toward post-familialism: economically advanced countries are embracing new social models that move away from family as the central organizing unit of society. This creates a more atomized and less cohesive society. As families move to the suburbs, large, urban city spaces become less child friendly.[59]

57. Kearney, *Two-Parent Privilege*, 139.
58. Goldberg, "There's Something about Marriage," 3:00.
59. Kotkin et al., *Rise of Post-Familialism*.

Others argue that demographic decline will hollow out the workforce, harm the economy, and slow the pace of innovation.[60] The double whammy of declining fertility and an aging society will strain the public social safety net as there are fewer taxpaying workers to support the growing demand for services. Despite the significant impact changing demographics will have on life in North America, few policymakers are willing to consider or publicly acknowledge the problem of declining marriage and family.

Acknowledging the evidence connecting family structure and challenges such as crime and poverty or demographic decline has proved to be controversial and divisive. The personal nature of family formation and the potential risk of being misunderstood as condemning families or particular communities has made the space difficult to navigate. Yet ignoring the evidence does little to strengthen communities.

We should be concerned about the growing economic and social divides along family structure lines. And we should be equally concerned about the challenges young adults face in forming the stable families they desire. Unfortunately, compared with the United States and the United Kingdom, in Canada we have too few conversations in the public square about the role of family structure in well-being and the marriage advantage. We need more conversations guided by good research.

---

60. Kotkin et al., *Rise of Post-Familialism*.

# 3

# Changing Marriage: The Trade Offs

THUS FAR WE'VE PRESENTED the idea that marriage has a more robust meaning and role in public life than most imagine. We've said the soulmate, "you complete me" model of marriage is too thin and impoverished to sustain a beautiful vision for the institution, one worthy of joining. Proposals for things like short-term marriage in law pull at the essential stitching around marriage. The long-term ideal of marriage is indisputably at the core of what marriage is and why we both want and need to have it in our lives. But what else is at the core?

It is true that institutions are not immutable, nor would we want them to be. All institutions shift and change over time. The language around social institutions likewise changes with their evolving purpose and needs. Here we raise some important questions: What are the essential elements that hold marriage together? What are the central, core functions of marriage? How may we ensure the center of marriage holds so that marriage can thrive and continue offering social goods like stability, longevity, connection, and the care of children? Which parts of this institution can change while the center holds?

In this chapter, we examine some of the forces stretching marriage. We invite you to consider the ways in which these forces have shaped modern marriage. We are considering the ways in which these trends have pulled at the center of marriage and the consequences of these forces. Typically, no trend is wrong wholesale, to be cast onto the rubbish heap of history. Rather we prefer to acknowledge trade-offs. In culture, progress can often mean that an advance in one area means regression in another; in other words, with a positive also comes a negative. This concept of trade-offs is often referenced in economic matters as opportunity costs. Very simply, if we sanction one form of marriage, it means we lose the opportunity to sanction something different. Marriage, in a sense, cannot be all things to all people. All too often we fail to see and name those trade-offs.[1]

## Feminism and the Sexual Revolution

In discussing trade-offs in the changing institution of marriage, there is likely no movement with greater impact than feminism. Feminism is an ideology that has changed much over centuries and continues to evolve. At a popular level, feminism may be described as an ideology that promotes women's choices, equality, and opportunity. Yet what feminism is and who gets to define it remain hotly contested. Today, we see a battle for what feminism is and, more to the point, what it ought to be. The result is that we see women today adding adjectives to feminism: freedom feminism, maternal feminism, sex-realist feminism, and so on. There are thus many "feminisms," and no one definition of feminism suits every feminist.[2]

---

1. Politicians are particularly reluctant to acknowledge trade-offs, instead naming "program *x*" as the latest, greatest consequence-free program in the history of the country. This may be the result of a prevailing focus on the short term. As regards laws and policies affecting marriage, this means politicians will likely be the last place to consider a nuanced approach to this institution of civil society.

2. See Leah Libresco Sargeant at OtherFeminisms.com; Sommers, *Freedom Feminism*; or the "sex-realist feminists" at FairerDisputations.org as examples of the many feminisms that currently compete for our attention.

Many manifestations of feminism oppose marriage, an opposition that has stretched and pulled at the concept of marriage as an institution, with some advocates calling for the end of marriage altogether. This stream of feminism has failed. After all, marriage stubbornly persists. But the arguments have seeped into popular culture, public policy, and the law.[3]

At the same time, a new, modern movement within feminism may hold the key to helping restore interest and confidence in marriage. How so? The answer lies in different historical attitudes feminists have held toward marriage and family over centuries. Today's modern, ascendant feminism has largely rejected marriage, but it was not always so—and it need not be so in the future.

Negative sentiments toward marriage reign supreme among feminists and have made their way into the popular consensus. Simone de Beauvoir, writing in *The Second Sex* in 1949, said this: "It has been said that marriage diminishes man, which is often true; but almost always it annihilates woman."[4] And, "The tragedy of marriage is not that it fails to assure woman the promised happiness . . . but [that] it mutilates her; it dooms her to repetition and routine. . . . Her life is virtually finished forever."[5]

Beauvoir is hardly alone in these views. A long list of feminists have communicated a range of negative and polemical views of marriage. Andrea Dworkin asserted that marriage evolved out of and helps to mainstream rape. Kate Millett's opposition to marriage led her to celebrate "[the] end of traditional sexual inhibitions and taboos, particularly those that threaten patriarchal monogamous marriage: homosexuality, 'illegitimacy,' adolescent, pre- and extramarital sexuality."[6] Finding feminists in the past fifty years who hate marriage is easier than shooting fish in a barrel. This hatred, however, is built out of a fundamental misunderstanding not only

---

3. One example is the unanticipated outcomes on marriage via the effect of feminist thought on child support guidelines after a divorce in Canada. See Allen, "Canada's Child Support Guidelines."
4. Beauvoir, *Second Sex*, 477.
5. Beauvoir, *Second Sex*, 478.
6. Doherty, "What Kate Did," para. 10.

of marriage but also of women and women's aspirations for family life (not to mention men's motivations for the same).

Admittedly, some strands of feminist opposition to marital law were not plucked out of thin air. Feminists opposed laws of coverture, which in the English common-law tradition removed individual rights from women, placing them instead under the "cover" of their husbands. For these feminists, coverture left married women little or no legal or economic remedy from a bad or abusive marriage.[7] We can acknowledge alongside feminists that the ideal good marriage is not the reality for everyone. Just as it is not hard to find feminists with a disdain for marriage, it is also not hard to find abuses of the ideals for marriage, examples that throw fuel on the feminist fire aiming to burn marriage to the ground.

That said, some early feminists were able to speak to problems like coverture without throwing the baby out with the bathwater. Early founding feminist Mary Wollstonecraft, writing in the late 1700s, was profoundly pro-marriage and pro-family, seeing these as the highest of virtuous callings. For her, the rights of women were paramount in every domain, politically, legally, and domestically. And she was sex blind in her belief that the home was an important ground for breeding virtue in men as well as women. "Wollstonecraft believed that domestic affections should take priority for both men and women, as therein lay the happiness of the couple, their children, and the world into which well-loved, self-possessed persons would go," writes Erika Bachiochi.[8] Bachiochi explains how Wollstonecraft thought that "ordinary domestic life was a gift to the world" and further that "the welfare of society is not built on extraordinary exertions."[9]

---

7. Opposition to coverture is reasonable; however, some feminists ignore data showing marriage is protective. Research shows cohabiting relationships are more violent than marital ones. See Kenney and McLanahan, "Cohabiting Relationships More Violent." Further, feminist disdain for marriage has led to exaggerated claims of male-on-female violence. Sources reveal "gender symmetry in partner violence" and a "conflict of theory and data." See Straus, "Denying the Evidence"; Dutton and Nicholls, "Gender Paradigm."

8. Bachiochi, *Rights of Women*, 36.

9. Bachiochi, *Rights of Women*, 38.

## CHANGING MARRIAGE: THE TRADE OFFS

Wollstonecraft wrote *A Vindication of the Rights of Woman* in 1792. By the time of the women's rights convention in Seneca Falls, New York, in 1848, the women's movement was growing, becoming more influential but also more fractured. A shift in thinking would occur among a minority of suffragists who came to rely more heavily on John Locke and John Stuart Mill. "These more radical suffragists, most notably Elizabeth Cady Stanton, traded in Wollstonecraft's prioritization of the virtuous fulfillment of familial and social obligations for Locke's more individualistic and abstract conception of rights as protective of 'self-ownership,'" writes Bachiochi.[10]

This shift corresponded with a change in the way families earned their livelihoods. Some scholars point to the fact that work moved outside the home during the Industrial Revolution, both for men and women. This marked the start of a rift between public and private life and also between work and home. The very word "economy" actually comes from the Greek word *oikonomia*, which referred for centuries to the management of and production in a household. After the Industrial Revolution, work and home would be more sharply divided, with married men and women having little concept of a home economy. Today's realities bear this out: witness the many of us today who entirely vacate our home for schools and workplaces, day in and day out, leaving neighborhoods empty during working hours.

Today the legal doctrine of coverture no longer exists. We have greatly increased women's opportunities. Even so, some historians paint a much more nuanced picture than feminist studies departments of the realities of life for women while coverture was the legal norm. The working partnership between husbands and wives left little room for prejudice against women, who, while legally subject to laws of coverture, in practice were highly regarded and important contributors to the household economy. Speaking of life in the agrarian home, historian Alice Clark writes, "Women could hardly have been regarded as mere dependents on their husbands when the clothing for the whole

---

10. Bachiochi, *Rights of Women*, 67.

I . . . DO?

family was spun by their hands."[11] Reading almost any account of pioneer existence in the 1800s, whether in Canada or the United States, will highlight the absolute necessity of men, women, and children working—very hard—together.

As the movement toward work outside the home increased, early feminists were successful in advocating for labor laws, which recognized the distinct needs of women as mothers. This included advocating for benefits and protections that would allow women to live as mothers raising children. This was rightly viewed as an accomplishment. William Gairdner, author of *The War Against the Family*, writes, "The finest social accomplishment of the 19th century was its success in getting the women and children out of the factory, off the streets, and into the schools as well as the homes, which is where mothers wanted to be and where everyone wanted children to be."[12] Tocqueville observed, "The Americans . . . have carefully separated the functions of man and of woman [into clearly distinct spheres of action] so that the great work of society may be better performed."[13] This division of labor was the progressive advancement of its day.

Marriage, for some women's advocates, far from oppressing and constraining women, was a partnership in which both worked for the good of their family. Unfortunately, the current feminist lens never ceases to view women as oppressed in or outside marriage, even where no coverture laws exist. This prevailing view makes it well-nigh impossible to explore the ways in which marriage evolved to "oppress" men. Who among us is familiar with the view that men, who might otherwise "sow their seed" without taking responsibility, are brought into the family enterprise by the "limitations" imposed by lifelong marriage? Marriage, something modern feminists fail to note, makes demands of men just as it does of women.

11. Bachiochi, *Rights of Women*, 84.
12. Gairdner, *War against the Family*, 80.
13. Tocqueville, as cited in Bachiochi, *Rights of Women*, 74.

## CHANGING MARRIAGE: THE TRADE OFFS

By the 1870s, some feminists had begun to campaign that women must work outside the home to achieve independence. Bachiochi writes:

> Some [women's rights advocates] even expressly denounced the assumption inherent in decades of joint property advocacy; that both the public and private spheres were of equal value, committed interdependently to the wellbeing of the family. Rather, to these more radical elements, cultural efforts to extol home labor would keep women content in their subordinate position, uninterested in freeing themselves from such burdens to pursue opportunities in the public sphere.[14]

By the twentieth century, feminists advocating for the virtue of marriage and family had lost their currency in debate and politics. By mid-century these feminist voices were engulfed in the sexual revolution, which gave high priority to sexual freedom, not the sexual constraint marriage espoused, alongside demands for the overthrow of all tradition. If we look at trends across the Western world at this time, a broader theme was revolution. In a period when calls for the overturning of all societal institutions grew louder and louder, it became more difficult to maintain a posture of openness to the good things from the past, like marriage. Of course, maintaining a posture of respect for other institutions was just as difficult; many people stopped trusting the government and ceased going to places of worship in this time frame as well. David Frum asserts that it was in the 1970s when "the ideas of the sexual revolution were absorbed as the common property of humanity."[15] And within that framework, marriage was fatally named as oppressor. With a battle cry of total revolution, marriage was thrown overboard as a patriarchal norm. Seeing marriage as a virtuous institution faded from sight in the rearview mirror.

Today's ascendant feminism finds its philosophical foundation in Marxism. And while many view Marxism as being oriented toward community and those things we hold in common ("This

14. Bachiochi, *Rights of Women*, 88.
15. Frum, *How We Got Here*, xxiii.

land is our land, this land is your land . . ."), this is not actually the case. For the opposite is true in practice. A core tenet of Marxism is the atomization of people and the removal of individuals from natural communities, of which marriage is the foundation. Isolated individuals can more easily become people without loyalties, more willing to become subservient to the state as their new community. It is with this view of extreme individualization in mind that philosopher Scott Yenor writes of feminism as hostile to marriage and family: "Insofar as feminism advocates for independence, it is hostile to the claims of motherhood, fatherhood, and marriage, since all of these imply the presence of love and dependence."[16]

Feminism is not the only "ism" to stretch marriage. Socialism, individualism, and the rejection of self-sacrifice—a requirement not just in marriage but primarily in having children—do so as well. However, the ascendant form of feminism has been all too happy to attempt to eradicate marriage instead of viewing it as a partnership that brings men and women together for the good of raising children and the creation of a home economy. Earlier feminists, seeking consideration for women as wives, mothers, and caregivers at the start of the twentieth century, made up an important and respectable current of feminism that ran alongside other streams. We have reached a point when it is time for the pendulum to swing back to this more family-friendly form.

There is strong evidence this is happening. Many self-described feminists are speaking out against the sexual revolution and in favor of marriage. No better example exists than Louise Perry, who wrote *The Case against the Sexual Revolution*, which includes a whole chapter called "Marriage Is Good." Perry is a self-described feminist, and her biography includes campaigning against "male sexual violence." It would be difficult to pigeonhole her as a religious campaigner for traditional values. And yet, she argues that, in light of the evidence, the diminishing of marriage has been destructive for women in particular, her target audience. So many strands of feminism have never included any concern for caring for children, and the duty that comes with

16. Yenor, *Family Politics*, 193.

having them, for both men and women. And while fertility rates are collapsing around the globe, having children remains an important aspirational goal, one that is best done within marriage for women, men, and children, as we argued above. Volumes of research speak to this, as do the testimonies of generations of now adult children raised outside marriage.

The extent to which feminism can embrace marriage and family as legitimate and fulfilling choices for women and men today will mark its success for the future. Certainly, there are already plenty of women who believe this is possible. This means we can end a section on feminism's dire impact on marriage on a hopeful note—we may in fact be turning a corner away from feminism's hostility toward marriage.

## Normalizing Divorce

No one gets married thinking their relationship will end in divorce. It is an unintended outcome, and one with negative consequences even when it is necessary. While divorce most often starts out as a solution, all too often it becomes increasingly acrimonious as the process unfolds. The normalization of divorce involved many factors. However, one of the most significant shifts took place when divorce law was reformed in the twentieth century, leading to a substantial increase in divorce. For all its faults, the pre-divorce reform era understood the significance and seriousness of dissolving a marriage.

While legal changes to divorce may have been intended to make the process less harmful in theory, this divorce revolution has in practice pulled at the center of marriage in consequential ways. A culture that overwhelmingly accepts divorce undervalues the permanency of marriage. It makes the words "till death do us part" ring hollow. It's also not entirely clear that easier access to divorce has actually made divorce less traumatic.

The divorce revolution marks a major trade-off in how we understand marriage. On the positive side, there's an easy way out of a marriage. On the negative side, people leave salvageable marriages.

Where divorce laws changed, an increase in divorce followed in both Canada and the United States. Increased divorce erodes the sense of permanency of marriage. "Why get married if half of marriages end in divorce" is a sentiment we often hear.

In many jurisdictions prior to the divorce revolution, one needed to be found at fault in order to divorce. Abuse, abandonment, or adultery had to be proved or admitted. Typically, the spouse not at fault would have to grant permission for the divorce. The introduction of no-fault divorce either added no-fault reasons such as "irreconcilable differences" or removed the burden of fault to acquire a divorce. Proponents of no-fault divorce believed this would make the process less acrimonious.

Ronald Reagan approved no-fault divorce in California in 1969 when he was governor. Thirty-seven states would follow, enacting such laws throughout the 1970s. Though the pathways to no-fault divorce were different in Canada and the United States, the effects have looked remarkably similar in both countries.

In Canada, previous to the 1968 Divorce Act, provincial law governed divorce in most provinces, but a few jurisdictions required a private act of Parliament to secure a divorce. Written notice of the intent to petition the government for a divorce was required in the *Canada Gazette* and two regional newspapers prior to seeking a divorce from Parliament. The 1968 act empowered provincial supreme courts to hear divorce cases, expanded the grounds for divorce to include "permanent marriage breakdown," and eliminated divorce by act of Parliament.[17]

With the introduction of "permanent marriage breakdown" to the already stated fault-based causes such as adultery, desertion, and cruelty, the 1968 act introduced the key element of no-fault divorce, which is the ability to unilaterally dissolve a marriage. Amendments to the Divorce Act in 1985 made it easier and more efficient to obtain a unilateral divorce by further relaxing conditions for divorce under the Divorce Act. Couples would be permitted to cite marriage breakdown as the reason

---

17. Douglas, "Divorce Law in Canada," under "Background and Analysis: A. History of Divorce Law in Canada," para. 4.

for divorce following one year of separation. The reform also allowed for joint filing for divorce that in some cases could ease the process and avoid a court appearance if other matters were agreed on, such as the division of property. Another significant aspect of the 1985 reform was the reduction of time between the divorce judgment and the judgment taking effect. This period was shortened from two years to thirty-one days.

Tracking the development of no-fault divorce in the United States is more complex, as legislative changes were made at the state level. Some states enacted abrupt changes, while other states made minor amendments to at-fault divorce law. For example, a state might have significantly reduced the period of separation required before a divorce.[18] While the legal changes happened in different ways across the states, what is clear is that a significant increase in divorce followed the rapid changes in divorce laws. The US divorce rate more than doubled between 1960 and 1980.[19]

The legal changes to divorce reflected a shifting cultural mood. Certainly, the 1960s and 1970s were a time of significant cultural change, including moving away from traditional institutions. Still, it's not entirely clear whether the law followed the culture or the culture followed the law. Either way, legal changes to divorce were met with increased divorce.

An act of Parliament for a divorce certainly sounds archaic to modern ears. And some aspects of divorce reforms did reduce harms inflicted by the process. For example, Governor Ronald Reagan, signing in no-fault divorce in California, did so at least in part because, in order for his own first marriage to end in 1948, his former spouse had needed to accuse him of mental cruelty.[20] At the same time, "no-fault divorce" doesn't mean there isn't fault, only that the courts will not seek to find it.[21]

18. Vlosky and Monroe, "Effective Dates."

19. Wilcox, "Evolution of Divorce," para. 2.

20. Even with no-fault divorce, false and exaggerated allegations against the other spouse are still alive and well today. This is particularly true in custody battles for children.

21. Some jurisdictions may still use fault to prescribe support and custody guidelines in a divorce.

While making divorces less painful is a worthy goal, the problem is that divorce is fundamentally an acrimonious event. Divorce is both the result and the source of conflict. Under these conditions, is the expectation of no-fault divorce to diminish acrimony reasonable? We all know cases of divorce where both parties intended to split amicably, but it did not turn out that way. The "good divorce" is something of a myth. It's a term that reflects a desire for less acrimonious marital dissolution for the sake of children and represents an admirable aspirational goal. However, it is also something of an oxymoron.

Divorce is the fracturing of a relationship intended to be permanent. Even in low-conflict divorces, children face the reality of living between two homes in most cases and the loss of having their parents together. Certainly, there are scenarios where divorce is necessary, but it still involves fracture and loss. An amicable divorce is better than one in which acrimony reigns. Yet the "good divorce" risks glossing over the grief of broken relationships, particularly for children who have no say in the matter.

During the early days of the divorce revolution, some experts suggested that no-fault divorce would free people from unhappy relationships in order to form better-quality marriages. Survey evidence suggests that marital happiness actually decreased following no-fault divorce.[22] Subsequent marriages following divorce also have a higher likelihood of ending in divorce, compared with first marriages.

One can hope that all divorces would be low conflict, but the people involved face significant challenges. Where children are involved, divorce ends the marriage but doesn't end the relationship, as negotiations over shared child-rearing are common, now often conducted without trust or goodwill. The irony is that divorced adults with children remain tied to one another through their kids. During the early years of no-fault divorce, experts spoke of how resilient children are as a way of consoling adults. The weight of evidence of the impact on children, however, suggests that even when divorce is unavoidable and necessary, it is never good.

22. Wilcox, "Evolution of Divorce," para. 23.

In general, children of divorce are more likely to experience negative outcomes, including behavioral issues and lower educational attainment.[23] It's possible that the pre-divorce parental conflict contributes to poor outcomes, but at this point there is a solid body of evidence that divorce itself harms children.[24] Sociologist Paul Amato argues that about two thirds of divorces are low conflict, where marital struggle and discord may not be fully detected by children. These divorces still affect children because the split is often unforeseen by the children.[25]

Evidence suggests that children who experience a divorce are more likely to divorce as an adult, especially if their partner also experienced a divorce as a child. Similarly, adults who experienced divorce as a child are much more likely to cohabit instead of getting married.[26] No-fault divorce is not altogether as easy and blameless as the term implies. It is most often unilateral, meaning one person in the marriage is blindsided by the other's desire for divorce. It takes two to get married, but one person alone can leave a marriage.

Harry Benson, research director for the Marriage Foundation in the United Kingdom, describes his own story as one that might well have ended in a no-fault or, better put, unilateral divorce. He hadn't realized how unhappy his wife was until she gave him an ultimatum to change or their marriage would be over in a year's time. "For me, it was panic stations, a bolt from the blue. I thought I was about to lose the children I loved. I never saw it coming and, worse, I had absolutely no idea what to do."[27] He describes how six months into the ultimatum he still wasn't getting it—he wasn't changing, or at least not for the right reasons. The motivation of keeping the kids

23. McLanahan and Sandefur, *Growing Up*; Kearney, *Two-Parent Privilege*, 53–54; Wilcox, "Evolution of Divorce."

24. Wallerstein et al., *Unexpected Legacy of Divorce*; Ross and Mirowsky, "Parental Divorce, Life-Course Disruption"; Boccia et al., "Parental Divorce in Childhood"; Cherlin et al., "Effects of Divorce."

25. Wilcox, "Evolution of Divorce."

26. Diekmann and Schmidheiny, "Intergenerational Transmission of Divorce."

27. Benson, "Hopelessly Unhappy?," para. 17.

wasn't helping him be the husband his wife needed. His wife continued to give him pointers as to what she needed him to change. And he did. They are still together, two more children and decades later. But the ultimatum his wife gave and the guidance that accompanied it toward change is all too rare. For many, divorce papers are the starting and end point all in one. One party is done, and the other is only just getting acquainted with the idea that the marriage is rocky. Today, Benson says he was not a good husband to his wife at this time. Back then, he took a different view. This is not to say Benson's case is prescriptive. But it does highlight how the serving of divorce papers can be tragically unexpected and that rebuilding a marriage takes time.

None of this is to say that anyone should be compelled to stay in a marriage. Rather, we are highlighting that so-called no-fault divorce is not necessarily easier, and making divorce easier for some has contributed to a culture in which marriage is less permanent for all. In fact, there is evidence of a social network effect—that is, having close friends and relatives who divorce is correlated with an increased risk of divorce.[28] This is called *divorce contagion*. In short, a culture where divorce is prevalent can lead to more divorce. Mandy, age thirty-seven, speaks of learning about her sister's divorce when it was already a fait accompli. "I asked my sister—who did you consult? How did you make this decision? Only to learn that she had been immersed in a small group of friends in which three of the four were divorced or divorcing." After it was too late, the sister regretted her actions. Now Mandy, who was not consulted in the first place, offers childcare and other supports.

To conclude, some people were hurt without easy access to divorce, but others have likewise been hurt in a culture that broadly accepts divorce and practices it widely. The hurt parties include the children but also the spouses, whose lives must be rebuilt, and their communities, who must accept and live with the new realities of separate homes and typically diminished financial assets. Even those who applaud no-fault divorce would

---

28. Morin, "Is Divorce Contagious?"

be wise to recognize that it compels communities to step up and support those now divided families more.

## The (Mostly) Good News of a Declining Divorce Rate

You've likely heard that half of marriages end in divorce. While that may have been true decades ago in the United States, it isn't the case currently. There are a number of methods for measuring the prevalence of divorce. The frequently quoted 50-percent figure is a method that relies on cohort data to develop a probability of a married couple divorcing over a set period of time, usually about three decades. By this measure, about 34 percent of marriages ended in divorce in pre-pandemic Canada.[29]

The divorce rate is far from 50 percent, which illustrates a decline in the divorce rate, particularly during the pandemic years. The thirty-year total divorce rate is a projection, and while it's the rate most often reported in popular media, there are other divorce rate measures that can be helpful in understanding trends in divorce.

Another way to measure divorce is to count the number of marriages that dissolve in a given year. This can provide an interesting historical perspective when looking at data year after year and can alert us to changing trends. For example, the number of divorces in Canada slowly rose after the Second World War, then increased dramatically after 1968. This spike corresponds with the introduction of the 1968 Divorce Act, which eased the restrictions around getting divorced. Another spike in the number of divorces occurred following reforms to the Divorce Act in 1985.

Another option is the crude divorce rate (CDR), which measures the number of divorces per 1,000 people. The CDR is often used for international comparison, but the rate can be influenced by demographic shifts such as the age structure of a population.

A similar measure enumerates the number of persons who divorce per 1,000 *married* people—the population at risk for

29. Statistics Canada, "Number of Divorces."

divorce. This is sometimes called the refined or marital divorce rate. By this measure, divorce has dramatically declined in both Canada and the United States over the last number of decades. Divorce declined in the United States from about 20 per 1,000 population in 1991 to 14.9 per 1,000 population in 2019.[30] The Canadian rate fell from 12.7 per 1,000 married people in 1991 to 7.5 per 1,000 in 2019.[31] Divorce rates tumbled in both countries during the COVID-19 pandemic, when lack of access to the court system contributed to the decline.

Declining divorce rates are good for marriage. Divorce is devastating financially and emotionally on adults and children. While declining divorce rates are positive, the good news is tempered by observations like those from Statistics Canada that the decline reflects the changing demographics around marriage. Young adults have a higher risk of divorce but are increasingly living together outside marriage. As a result, less divorce-prone older adults account for a larger portion of the married population. As we will illustrate later, when marriage becomes less common, those who do choose to marry may have certain traits or characteristics that result in a lower likelihood of divorce.[32] As the demographics of married couples have shifted, divorcing couples today are a little older and their marriages tend to endure a little longer before ending in dissolution, compared with divorcing couples in the past.[33] Celebration of the decline in divorce rates should be tempered. A closer look at the trend reveals that the overall decline in marriage, particularly among young adults, has contributed to the decline in divorce.

30. W. Wang, "US Divorce Rate."
31. Statistics Canada, "Fifty-Year Look," 5.
32. Statistics Canada, "Fifty-Year Look," 6.
33. Statistics Canada, "Fifty-Year Look," 7–8.

## The Growing Prevalence of Cohabitation

Is marriage more than a piece of paper? We can consider this question in the context of the growth of common-law relationships, which is a significant narrative within the North American marriage storyline. About 13 percent of couples in the United States live in cohabiting rather than married relationships, while nearly 23 percent of Canadian couples cohabit.[34] This trend not only reveals the shifting sexual mores in Western culture but also illustrates the changing attitudes toward marriage. Daniel, age eighty-three, tells us that for him marriage marked a step into adulthood: "I didn't know any couples who lived together outside of marriage, and I didn't know anyone who got divorced." Contrast that with Sarah, age fifty, who got married at age twenty-nine after living with her boyfriend for over a year. What is a normal part of our lives today was not considered an option by previous generations.

Couples enter common-law relationships with a variety of intentions. For some, it's a good-for-now arrangement, while others live together as a step toward marriage. Still others view common-law arrangements as an equivalent to marriage but without the piece of paper. Few people realize that living together before getting married increases the risk of divorce rather than offering a better chance at a successful marriage.[35]

Few states offer legal protections for cohabiting couples, particularly around dissolution of a relationship. In Canada, however, almost all provinces grant some legal protection to common-law couples, but typically fewer than married couples, around the division of assets on a relationship's end.

For many couples, the absence of a legal commitment with the ability to more easily step out of a common-law relationship is a desirable feature. It's no great surprise, then, that common-law relationships are more prone to break up.

---

34. US calculations by authors based on Gryn et al., "Married Couple Households," fig. 3; United States Census Bureau, "Census Bureau Releases"; Statistics Canada, "State of the Union."

35. Stanley and Rhoades, *What's the Plan?*

There are functional differences between common-law relationships and marriage. One example lies in financial habits. Common-law couples are less likely to pool their income, which can affect wealth creation.[36] One study shows a correlation between the number of incidents of cohabitation experienced prior to marriage and decreasing net worth.[37] Cohabitation and, particularly, serial cohabitation, delay the ability to build financial assets.[38]

Further, evidence suggests that common-law relationships are more prone to intimate-partner violence and child abuse.[39] This is a particular concern when these relationships involve unrelated adults living in the child's home. The risk of abuse is up to ten times higher for children who co-reside with a parent's partner who is unrelated to them.[40]

While it is difficult to hear and talk about, children are often affected by their parents' romantic decisions. Canadian data from two cohorts of the National Longitudinal Survey of Children and Youth published in 1999 showed that 63 percent of children born to cohabiting parents experienced their parents' separation by age ten, compared with 14 percent of their peers born to married parents who never cohabited.[41] Canadian research has found that separated men from common-law relationships are less likely to keep contact with their kids, compared with divorced men.[42]

Of course, we all know common-law couples who have lived in loving and successful long-term relationships. In the aggregate, however, the data suggest that common-law relationships are more prone to some negative outcomes, compared with marriage. The lower level of commitment required and sometimes desired in a common-law relationship may contribute to these risks.

---

36. Hamplova et al., "One Pot or Two Pot."
37. Britt-Lutter et al., "Financial Implications of Cohabitation," 40.
38. Britt-Lutter et al., "Financial Implications of Cohabitation," 39–40.
39. Nock, "Comparison of Marriages."
40. Sedlak et al., *Fourth National Incidence Study*, 12.
41. Department of Justice, "Selected Statistics," fig. 10.
42. Galt, "Changing Face," para. 10.

The trend toward more couples starting out together in common-law relationships, and more couples choosing to forgo marriage altogether, raises an important question. With less social pressure to marry, is common law becoming the new marriage?

Some scholars have assumed that the increasing portion of couples living together before marriage would result in the association between premarital cohabitation and later divorce dissipating over time. This hasn't been the case. A recent study found that while premarital cohabitation is correlated with less divorce in the first few years of marriage, those who lived together before marriage are more likely to divorce over the long haul, compared with those who didn't.[43] This has led some scholars to quip that living together before marriage is good preparation for divorce—a jarring statement, given many live together precisely because they think it provides good preparation for marriage.

As cohabitation becomes more common, it is fair to ask if this family form will replace marriage. Is it possible that cohabitation will essentially function as the new marriage?

The province of Quebec provides interesting insights into this question, as the province has one of the highest cohabitation rates in the world. There, the portion of cohabiting relationships accounts for nearly 36 percent of all census families.[44] In fact, 43 percent of all cohabiting couples in Canada live in Quebec. This is in spite of the fact that Quebec offers the fewest legal protections for cohabiting couples, compared with the other provinces.

---

43. Rosenfeld and Roesler, "Cohabitation Experience."

44. Statistics Canada defines *census family* as a "married couple and the children, if any, of either and/or both spouses; a couple living common law and the children, if any, of either and/or both partners; or a parent of any marital status in a one-parent family with at least one child living in the same dwelling and that child or those children. All members of a particular census family live in the same dwelling. Children may be biological or adopted children regardless of their age or marital status as long as they live in the dwelling and do not have their own married spouse, common-law partner or child living in the dwelling. Grandchildren living with their grandparent(s) but with no parents present also constitute a census family" (Statistics Canada, "Census Family," para. 1).

With such a high portion of cohabiting couples, Quebec has one of the lowest portions of married census families, at about 48 percent. There are many significant factors that contribute to the social transformation of family life in Quebec; we will return to discuss them later. For now, we pause to consider what we may learn from the rapid growth of common-law relationships in the province.

Sociologists Céline Le Bourdais and Évelyne Lapierre-Adamcyk concluded in the mid-2000s that as cohabitation increased in Quebec, the stability of marriage decreased. At the same time, cohabiting unions appeared stabler than in the rest of Canada, but still less stable than marriage in Quebec or the rest of Canada.[45] Outside Quebec, they found that the increase in common-law couples resulted in more lower-commitment couples.[46]

Le Bourdais and Lapierre-Adamcyk were interested in how cohabiting couples functioned, compared with married couples. They found that cohabiting couples in Quebec were still less likely to pool income, compared with married couples, but more likely to share in paid and unpaid labor.[47]

As we just noted, Canadian provinces outside Quebec offer various degrees of legal protections upon separation to cohabiting relationships. This has allowed economists to examine how these protections influence economic behavior. One study found that after the introduction of protections, there was an increase in men's earnings and working hours, but a decrease in working hours and earnings among women.[48] In short, increasing legal protections for cohabiting couples was associated with what we may think of as traditional divisions within marital behavior when it comes to paid work.

Another helpful observation is to examine the task of bearing and raising children. Are cohabiting couples as likely to have and

---

45. Le Bourdais and Lapierre-Adamcyk, "Changes"; Menard, "What Makes It Fall Apart?"
46. Le Bourdais and Lapierre-Adamcyk, "Changes," 934.
47. Le Bourdais and Lapierre-Adamcyk, "Changes," 939–40.
48. Groussé and Leturcq, "More or Less Unmarried."

raise children together as married couples? Answering this question provides further insight into whether common-law relationships are functionally replacing marriage.

An indirect indicator of how parenting is perceived in common-law relationships is to examine the living arrangements of children.[49] Looking at data from the 2021 Canadian Census, nearly as many children in Quebec live with common-law parents (38.9 percent) as with married parents (39.4 percent). When we look at the rest of Canada (excluding Quebec), 66.3 percent of children live in married-parent homes and 10.7 percent with common-law parents.[50] This illustrates the significant cultural differences in family life in Quebec, compared with the rest of the country.

Certainly, cohabitation has become a common family form in Quebec and is viewed as an arrangement in which to have children. The data would suggest, however, that even as cohabitation has become more stable in Quebec, it does not replicate the stability of marriage. We take a deeper dive into Quebec's distinct social culture later in this chapter.

## Same-Sex Marriage

Same-sex marriage was federally legislated in Canada in 2005 and in the United States ten years later, in 2015. The introduction of same-sex marriage remains a shift not only in how we practice marriage but also in how we understand its purpose. Same-sex marriage received—and in some ways, continues to receive—more attention than other consequential changes in how we consider marriage. While one would be hard pressed to find a person on the street with strong feelings about no-fault divorce or cohabitation, acceptance of same-sex marriage continues to serve as a litmus test for participation in public life and for whether a person is welcoming and respectful.

49. Le Bourdais and Lapierre-Adamcyk, "Changes," 936.

50. See table 1, "Portion of Children Aged 0 to 14 Living in Married, Common-law, and Lone-Parent Families, by Region, 2021," in Mitchell, "Canadian Children at Home."

No matter where one stands, removing the opposite-sex requirement in marriage remains a historic shift and provides a rare instance of public debate and dialogue reflecting the fact that marriage does indeed still matter.

Our intent here is not to relitigate the expansion of marriage to same-sex couples. Rather, it is to show that this is a significant change in the history of marriage and that this change, along with others before it, is also a case of trade-offs. Same-sex marriage is the result of changes to the institution and also portends further change. These points are controversial in a culture that views the introduction of same-sex marriage as an unmitigated good, and one without consequences. We believe, however, these questions are worth exploring by people of goodwill, because there are current debates about expanding marriage further, and there will likely be future ones too.[51]

First, a little bit on the time it took to arrive at a place of considering what marriage might be in an institutional framework. Back in 2004, I (Andrea) worked at *Toronto Life* magazine. I recall a brief conversation with another intern, who said he couldn't imagine why anyone would oppose same-sex marriage. The question was simmering in the background of daily life for those of us in journalism at the time. I remember thinking there might be reasons, but I couldn't think of any. I didn't pursue the topic any further. After all, I had done no work on the topic, and I knew what I was supposed to believe—and it was the view of my fellow intern in our tiny, windowless office.

In 2006, I applied to work at a Christian think tank called the Institute of Marriage and Family Canada, which would, for ten years, promulgate conservative Christian views using secular social science research in the public square. Hilariously, in the interview process for the job, I politely made it clear I was happy to address any issue *but* marriage. This was because I had no interest in being compelled to espouse any position in favor of man-woman marriage without knowing any logical justification behind it.

---

51. MacDonald, "Three Adults"; Taylor-Coleman, "Polyamorous Marriage."

Second, and relatedly, I was not keen on being portrayed as a bigot on the nightly news. I knew I held (and hold) no animus toward sexual minorities. But there was no wiggle room to dissent against the packaging of support for gay marriage as being the same thing as support for gay rights and, by extension, gay people. There were more than enough other family issues to keep me busy, and I remained focused on those.

The Institute of Marriage and Family was Christian, and having become a practicing Christian in my mid- to late twenties, I was (and remain) a Christian. No church I'd attended provided any information or reasoning for the historical Christian view—a view largely supported by major religions worldwide—that marriage is between a man and a woman. After all, the majority of marriages have been between heterosexuals even in societies where same-sex love has the same legitimacy as heterosexuality.[52] I mention this only because it would be wrong to assume that religious people, even those in the pews weekly today, hold a particularly informed view of marriage or that we've thought much about it. Some have, and certainly a huge body of theology on the subject exists, but I had not. So the journey began with considering marriage first as a secular policy issue, not a theological one, through the works of a range of scholars affiliated with all points on the political spectrum, including Isabel Sawhill, Andrew Cherlin, Linda Waite, Douglas Allen, Steven Nock, Kay Hymowitz, Jennifer Roback Morse, Elizabeth Marquardt, Glenn Stanton, and David Blankenhorn, among others.

This resulted in my own slow and wildly inconvenient transformation in thinking, away from an unfocused notion of marriage as purely about love and commitment regardless of sex and toward marriage as existing in an institutional framework, between one man and one woman. I came to understand that I had never seen this institutional framework as a pervasive cultural presence. The separation of sex, children, and marriage occurred in the 1960s, along with the first step of divorce reforms in Canada, before many of us members of Generation X were born.

52. Coontz, *Marriage, a History*, 28.

In the 2000s, legal cases were starting to make changes toward accepting same-sex marriage in Canada, but the general view of marriage was likely better encapsulated by the language in the legal argumentation. In 1995, the Supreme Court of Canada wrote about the case Egan v. Canada:

> Marriage has from time immemorial been firmly grounded in our legal tradition, one that is itself a reflection of long-standing philosophical and religious traditions. But its ultimate *raison d'être* transcends all of these and is firmly anchored in the biological and social realities that heterosexual couples have the unique ability to procreate, that most children are the product of these relationships, and that they are generally cared for and nurtured by those who live in that relationship. In this sense, marriage is by nature heterosexual. It would be possible to legally define marriage to include homosexual couples, but this would not change the biological and social realities that underlie the traditional marriage.[53]

Removing the opposite-sex requirement in marriage, like the change to broadly normalizing divorce before it, as we have observed, marks a major shift in the history of marriage. The intent here isn't to provide a history of how countries came to accept same-sex marriage but rather to point to the idea that this change is an outcome of prior change in how we consider marriage, as much as it portends any future changes about marriage. Only in a culture with a strongly held conviction that marriage is purely about love and companionship could such changes be made.

Indeed, same-sex marriage both flows from a soulmate model of marriage and reinforces it. Where institutional marriage intends to bind mothers and fathers to their children, the debate over the definition of marriage focused primarily on adult rights. Removing sex from the definition of marriage reduced the significance of biological parenthood and the number of adults who could claim parenthood of a child. Following same-sex marriage, our home province of Ontario passed legislation permitting multiple adults

---

53. As cited in McKay, "Confusion on the Hill," 31–32.

to enter a preconception agreement to share legal parenthood of yet-to-be-conceived children. The result is that children in Ontario can be born with more than two legal parents. Regardless of how one perceives this change, it is a direct legal descendant of removing the opposite-sex requirement in marriage.

Institutions shift over time, and some will argue that marriage has simply expanded to include a minority that has certainly faced discrimination. In Canada, same-sex married couples make up 0.4 percent of all couples, while common-law same-sex couples account for 0.7 percent of all couples.[54] In the United States, same-sex married couples make up about 1 percent of all couples, while unmarried same-sex couples account for about 0.8 percent of all couples.[55]

Some will argue that these small percentages make the change inconsequential. Some will further argue that, even if redefining marriage somehow reinforces the soulmate model, that model was already well entrenched. And that much is true—same-sex marriage became necessary because marriage had already shifted away from the institutional model.

During the marriage debates, some proposed a civil partnership model that affirmed equality rights to same-sex couples while maintaining an opposite-sex definition of marriage. The proposal was an attempt to navigate between the two sides, but ultimately failed. Marriage itself was redefined, a significant change in the history of marriage. The use of marriage as a tool to extend equality rights to same-sex couples meant that questions about the nature of parenthood, the relevance of sex and biology, and the purposes marriage rose up to fulfill were not addressed.

Today, any conversation about restricting marriage to opposite-sex partners is curtailed in public debate. Who curtails it? Certainly, social media is not the land of nuanced thought.

54. Calculations by authors from Statistics Canada, "Gender Diversity Status [2021]."

55. Calculations by authors from United States Census Bureau, "American Community Survey [2022]." See table 1, "Household Characteristics of Opposite-Sex and Same-Sex Couple Households," and table 2, "Household Characteristics of Same-Sex Couple Households by Relationship Type."

Politicians, policymakers, and journalists grandstand on the idea that an opposite-sex requirement to marriage is always bigoted. This unwillingness to allow freedom of thought is not limited to marriage but extends into many different moral issues. Another way to curtail thought is to compel people to come to premature decisions about outcomes in law and policy. One must first establish the facts of the matter for oneself. But in this domain, that is hard to do because there is an immediate push to consider what the consequences may be. Both those stridently in favor of same-sex marriage and those against it have ways of ensuring the majority simply stay quiet.

Neither does good come of discussions that immediately assume animus. Thankfully, there are scholars on both sides of the same-sex marriage debate who are able to maintain respect for others. Consider people like John Corvino, an advocate for same-sex marriage who wrote a book with Maggie Gallagher, an advocate for maintaining the opposite-sex requirement in marriage.[56]

In the past decades, our society has witnessed both the rapid evolution of ideas on sex and sexuality and the effects of living out the sexual revolution. These have been experienced both before and after the legalization of same-sex marriage. All of these changes, not limited to divorce or same-sex marriage but encompassing broader changes to dating/courtship, relationships, partnership, and even the definition of what it means to be a man or a woman, are worthy of robust conversation. Instead, the bandwidth for discussion has diminished. This means, too, that the bandwidth for even thinking about these things is narrower.

Canadian academic Paul Nathanson has thought publicly and charitably about marriage. In 2003, he argued that changing the definition of marriage changes its function, transforming marriage into a different institution. For Nathanson, "Discrimination to maintain marriage as it has long been identified should be allowed in view of the fact that marriage, as a universal institution and the essential cultural complement to biology, is prior

---

56. Corvino and Gallagher, *Debating Same-Sex Marriage*.

to all concepts of law."[57] He concludes that "redefining marriage would amount to a massive human experiment," much like the divorce revolution before it.[58] He also happens to be gay, which means his agenda cannot be to detract from his own personhood. But Canadians could be forgiven for never hearing his name, because to give him too much publicity would be to puncture a publicly held consensus that support for same-sex marriage is the same thing as support for equal rights for people who are gay. Publicly discussing these ideas ought not come with an immediate reprimand; it is the hallmark of thinking individuals to process new information through dialogue and questions, questions we all too often are scared to ask.

Same-sex marriage is the most electric of third-rail issues. This is not a book about same-sex marriage, for or against, but rather a book about marriage and its public benefits. The same-sex marriage debate pulls on and stretches the institutional understanding of marriage. Future debates about the definition of marriage will likely have to do with the number of partners. Numerous books, magazines, and news articles have recently made a case for the legitimacy of polyamorous relationships. Many of these opinions mirror the rights-based arguments for same-sex marriage. Of course, this isn't an argument that disqualifies same-sex marriage. But if marriage is a vehicle for equality, then arguments for making marriage sexless similarly apply to making marriage numberless.

All to say, changes in the definition of marriage require debate about the purpose of marriage. We'd ask whether changing marriage to include gay couples was the wrong tool (using marriage) for the right cause (removing discrimination against same-sex couples). The ideas underpinning the institutional model of marriage have little to do with rights and more to do with obligations. Thus, it should be perfectly possible to affirm someone's rights without altering the meaning of marriage, but that is not a conversation we are currently able to have.

57. Young and Nathanson, "All in the Family," para. 13.
58. Young and Nathanson, "All in the Family" para. 14.

I . . . DO?

## Monogamy

Monogamy has long been a core component of marriage. Will this remain true in the future? The question is not idle speculation. At the time of writing, the public's attitudes toward relationship trends like polyamory are shifting. There have been a spate of articles explaining and often promoting polyamorous lifestyles. We've laid out the philosophical underpinnings of why marriage is more than a romantic relationship and needs to be viewed institutionally. Now we turn our attention to discussing why monogamy should be a feature of marriage. After all, over the course of history, many societies have permitted polygamous families where men had multiple wives.

Canadian psychologist Sue Johnson notes that on the personal, psychological level, lifelong love remains an aspiration for many people, yet there is pessimism concerning the ability to achieve it.[59] She maintains, though, that it is achievable and, moreover, very important. Among other important aspects, she points to the production of the hormone oxytocin that facilitates bonding between partners. Research shows that simply thinking about one's partner increases oxytocin production. Johnson writes, "All of us may not be destined for a single, lifelong relationship, but we are naturally monogamous."[60] Put differently, humans are wired for pair bonding. The idea that vulnerable men and women need each other in different ways is a central reason why human beings created a way of living together that we would eventually call marriage.[61] Anthropologist Sarah Blaffer Hrdy points out that human beings are "born to attach."[62] Often the conversation about attachment is limited to that between mother and child, but we are born to attach as adult spouses as well.

---

59. Sue Johnson passed away on April 23, 2024. We will always be very grateful for her interest and input into our work.

60. Johnson, *Love Sense*, 125.

61. Wilson, *Marriage Problem*, 35.

62. Hrdy, *Mother Nature*, 383–93.

Adults are attached to one another for the purposes of staying together to raise children—a lengthy proposition.[63]

We may *be* pair-bonding creatures, but one has only to point to the propensity toward infidelity to note that monogamy may not *feel* natural. One can reject the argument that monogamy is natural and still acknowledge and accept the evidence that the adoption of monogamous marriage has been a societal advancement.

In polygynous societies, where one man is married to more than one woman, low-status males are less likely to find partners. These men are less future focused and more likely to engage in risky and antisocial behaviors like crime.[64] Also, the competition for wives results in men seeking younger women. Monogamy is linked with narrower age gaps between partners and greater equality for women. Married men tend to be more attentive to fathering and making a living—economic production. This is particularly true in monogamous marriage.[65]

Furthermore, people adopted monogamous marriage because it works and improves other aspects of shared institutions of governance, including democracy. Some scholars argue that "there is a statistical linkage between democratic institutions and normative monogamy."[66] The married man-woman family lays the foundation for individuals' participation in wider society.[67] Thus we see the arguments, arguments that we believe hold water, that monogamy is connected to more prosperous, stable, peaceful, and equal societies.

All this points toward the idea that relationship choices are never confined to the private domain. There are public ramifications to relationship choices, be they toward polygamy or polyamory. Nonmonogamous marriage, both plural marriage and open marriage, signals the continued shift away from child-centered marriage to adult-centered marriage. Gallup polls have shown that

63. Blankenhorn, *Future of Marriage*, 35.
64. Henrich et al., "Puzzle of Monogamous Marriage," 660.
65. Henrich et al., "Puzzle of Monogamous Marriage," 664.
66. Henrich et al., "Puzzle of Monogamous Marriage," 667.
67. Goldberg, *Suicide of the West*, 274.

increasing numbers of Americans think that polygamy is morally acceptable.[68] This speaks to an increasing lack of awareness about the benefits of stable, monogamous marriage. And it's not just polygamy. There are also trend lines pointing to a rising acceptance of polyamory, involving romantic relationships between more than two people. While it's difficult to measure how much that trend is growing, there are indicators that polyamory is rising in social acceptance.[69] As Hillary Clinton wrote in her 2006 book *It Takes a Village*, "Every society requires a critical mass of families that fit the traditional ideal, both to meet the needs of most children and to serve as a model for other adults who are raising children in difficult settings."[70] This leaves room for people also to fall outside the critical mass, provided there actually is a critical mass to sustain the majority, and that the minority remains a minority. Recent attempts to normalize polyamory, for example, suggest that some activists in that community wish for polyamory to be on moral par with that critical mass. But there's something of a delicate balancing act in maintaining the critical mass, and one question we may ask is what the tipping point may be, where an institution ceases to provide the benefits for which it has been known, simply because it is too radically altered or because the minority viewpoints became majority courses of action.

Public norms around marriage affirm and encourage the practice of monogamy. Whether monogamy is natural or not, it works; marriage reinforces the norm, guiding behavior toward social practices that benefit individuals and society. Although plural marriage has been evident throughout the historical record, the adoption of monogamous marriage represents progress.

---

68. "And while just 23 percent of Americans say that polygamy is morally acceptable, that's up from 7 percent in 2003" (Newport, "Untangling Americans' Complex Views," para. 3).

69. MacDonald, "Three Adults."

70. Clinton, *It Takes a Village*, 41.

## Rising Secularism: A Look at the Canadian Province of Quebec

"In practice, today's young people want to avoid, as long as possible, the duties and responsibilities of the married state. They may court their girlfriends for years without getting any closer to the goal. They do not live with the prospect of marriage in mind and thus neglect to prepare for it."[71] While this sounds like it could have been spoken today, it was written by Quebec priest Father Guillaume Lavallée in 1937.

Beautiful, more rural, home to amazing microbreweries, cathedrals, hydroelectricity, and more, more than a fifth of all Canadians call Quebec home. While you could swim to Quebec from Ottawa, Ontario, across the Ottawa River, it is more distant when it comes to two social trends important to a book about marriage. In this amazing province called Quebec, two forces, rising secularism and declining marriage rates, come together in a powerful way.

Indeed, Quebec is home to the lowest marriage rates in North America and the highest cohabitation rates in the G7. And it's home to some of the lowest levels of religious participation in Canada. Thus, it's worth unpacking whether these trends have relevance to the rest of North America. Not only this, but Quebec has adopted different family policy from the rest of Canada, in things like childcare and parental leave. In those areas, many North Americans often point to Quebec as an example to emulate.

Whether it's a case of emulating family policies or whether there is concern that we may have marriage rates that could dip as low as they are currently in Quebec, the issue is the same: Quebec is unique in its language, faith, history, and legal tradition, making it a tough place to emulate, good or bad. Religious participation is declining just about everywhere, but the reasons for the dramatic rise in secularism are different in Quebec.

Father Lavallée's quote above is an indication that declining respect for marriage has been a problem in Quebec for longer than we think. It's rare for a social trend to come out of the

---

71. Gauvreau, *Catholic Origins*, 80.

# I . . . DO?

blue. What many attribute to the Quiet Revolution, a series of significant social changes in Quebec dated to approximately the 1960s, actually hails from a time decades before that revolution began. Or perhaps it was quietly in progress for longer than we tend to think. Either way, caring what a priest says on the state of marriage in Quebec is something that could have happened only before the arrival of the Quiet Revolution and, with it, radical secularization in the province of Quebec.

The most recent Canadian census data highlight the distinctions:

> Among G7 countries, Canada has the highest share of couples that are living common law (23 percent), mainly due to the popularity of this type of union in Quebec—home to more than two-fifths (43 percent) of Canada's common-law couples. Excluding Quebec, the share of common-law couples in Canada would have been 17 percent in 2021.[72]

Quebec children are more likely than those in the rest of Canada to see the dissolution of their parents' relationship. Among children under the age of eighteen in Quebec, 23 percent have witnessed the divorce or separation of their parents, compared with the national average of 18 percent.[73]

We've mentioned that Quebec is unique linguistically and religiously. It also has a unique place within Canada's federation. It is the only province identifiable as its own "nation," a nation within the nation of Canada.[74] Quebec is linguistically isolated even today—a French island in English North America. And Quebec was religiously isolated as a bulwark of Roman Catholicism in a continent of (then) largely English Protestants. Perhaps because of this, the power of Roman Catholicism was far more pervasive and daily present in Quebeckers' lives since the arrival of Samuel de Champlain in 1603 than, say, the (not inconsequential) power of Presbyterianism elsewhere in English Canada.

72. Statistics Canada, "State of the Union," highlights, para. 6.
73. Statistics Canada, "How Many Children," map.
74. Anglin, "Country, Province, and Nation," para. 1.

From the earliest days, prior to the establishment of any government, the Roman Catholic Church took on very public responsibility for important areas like education, health care, and social services.[75] Religious power commingled with political power over decades, even centuries, with varying and debated effects on the strength of personal religious conviction among Quebeckers themselves.

Leading up to the Quiet Revolution, Quebec was also more rural and had more problems emerging from Depression-era unemployment. Youth unemployment was high in Quebec after the 1930s and did not bounce back in the same way as it did in English Canada.[76] At the same time, priests reportedly continued to exhort the faithful to be fruitful and multiply. (Consider that singer Céline Dion, who was born near Montreal in 1968, is the youngest of fourteen children.) Increasingly, economic conditions would make it difficult to support so many children with only one working (or, worse still, unemployed) father.

As recently as 1969, 98 percent of marriages in Quebec were religious, celebrated by a priest.[77] The loss of marriage there is thus a big change in recent history, first from a majority of partnerships being marriages (not cohabitations), and then also from a majority of these marriages being religiously celebrated rather than done by a civil authority. The Quiet Revolution was, in no small part, a rebellion against the Roman Catholic Church, which was (and still is) seen as an authoritarian killjoy. Quebeckers carry this mindset even today, which may contribute to the plummeting marriage and fertility rates specific to that province.

Going back centuries, Quebec had a different approach to marriage based in civil law, not common law. Quebec civil law established two types of contracts, one in which property was held in common, the other where it was not.[78]

75. Malvern, "Falling from Grace."
76. Gauvreau, *Catholic Origins*, 70.
77. Lincà, *Mariage civil au Québec*, 7.
78. Beaujot et al., "Family Policies in Quebec."

Quebec's Quiet Revolution in the 1960s would change the strictly religious character of the province. As the sexual revolution picked up steam across North America, the traditions, values, and even virtues associated with family were more and more consigned to a bygone era. The civil rights movement was rising in the United States, and the Cold War painted the backdrop for hot conflict across the globe. So it's not as though Quebec was unique in undergoing big, cultural, even revolutionary changes.

As the state took over the role once played by the church, living common-law, or *union de fait/union libre* in French, gained popularity. Interestingly, those who have lived in Quebec note that few seem to see the takeover of cohabitation as odd or undesirable. Some are even proud of it, seeing it as a sign of their being more advanced than the rest of Canada. They may refer to it as "Quebec's form of marriage," another reason why Quebec is distinct and separate.

Most scholars view declines in religion as preceding declines in family, but in her 2013 book on this issue, *How the West Really Lost God*, public intellectual Mary Eberstadt fleshes out the idea that declining families also contribute to the decline in religion. In short, these things are inextricably intertwined and complicated. Nowhere are these points more complicated than in a place like Quebec. Church authority was far more pervasive, but it's not clear that this always translated into an authentic spirituality for Quebeckers. Marriage was more prevalent in the Roman Catholic culture prior to the Quiet Revolution, but this too was changing as Quebeckers struggled with more individualistic approaches to the institution of marriage and the meaning of marriage in their lives.[79]

To add another layer of complexity, at the same time that roles for church and state were being negotiated within Quebec, so too was Quebec's place in Canada's federation. While Quebec is one of the founding provinces of Canada going back to the country's confederation in 1867, the tensions between French and English have always been strong (and some would argue have never really

---

79. Michael Gauvreau describes this at length in his book *Catholic Origins*.

disappeared). Quebec has long worked to assert its unique place within Canada in federal politics. Federal Members of Parliament sent to represent Quebeckers in Ottawa are currently almost half from a Quebec nationalist party, the Bloc Québécois. The main aim of the Bloc Québécois is to promote Quebec's sovereignty.

Where does that leave us with regard to family and especially marriage in Quebec today? A weak presence of religion does not spell good things for family life anywhere, and neither does it in Quebec. This is particularly true when we consider that more Quebec children witness the separation of their parents. It's also true, however, that common-law living arrangements look more like marriage in Quebec, with greater social acceptance toward the practice.

While marriage is not exclusively a religious institution, it is one that is supported in no small part by religious institutions. One friend recently complained that when he desires marital counseling or help, he simply cannot find it as a nonreligious Canadian. Many support networks intending to help marriages through troubled times are put in place by faith actors—church or parachurch organizations.

When the Roman Catholic Church was upended and replaced by the state in Quebec, it was a complete replacement; today's churches in Quebec are largely empty. Nowhere else in North America has any religion ever played the kind of outsized role that Roman Catholicism did in Quebec, staking territory as it did to defend not just religion but the very "nation" of Quebec. This may be why government ballooned more in Quebec than in other places, especially after the church vacated its key roles in education and health care.

All this means that a future for marriage similar to the story that statistics from Quebec tell seems unlikely. All too often we look to international examples to learn both about paths we wish to take and those we would rather not. The comparisons in this case are limited. It may seem feasible, since Quebec is geographically close. But Quebec's unique culture, religion, and history within Canada, let alone North America, or the Organisation for Economic Co-operation and Development, render such an outcome implausible.

## Living *La Vida Solo*: A Note about Lone Parenting

As marriage rates have declined in North America, the portion of children living with lone parents has increased. While this trend may influence how we think of marriage, the increase of lone-parent families is also clearly a result of the decline in a view in which marriage is considered important and necessary. Some adults are lone parents by choice, while others find themselves parenting alone due to life circumstances. However adults come to parenting on their own, lone parents face challenges that married couples are less likely to navigate.

While lone-parent families make up a sizeable portion of all families in North America, lone parenting is more prevalent in the United States, where 23 percent of children live in such a family (with no other adult present), compared with 15 percent in Canada. And this while Canada has greater portions of cohabiting families than does the United States.[80] In fact, the United States has the highest rate of children living with lone parents in the world.[81]

One of the significant narratives in the story of lone parenting in North America is the shift in the makeup of these families. Lone parenting was formerly a result of divorce and widowhood. More recently, an increasing number of lone parents have never married. For example, in Canada in 1971, just 7 percent of lone-parent families were never-married families. Four decades later, that portion had jumped to about 37 percent.[82] Currently in the United States, just over half of lone mothers have never married.[83]

Unfortunately, many children in lone-parent families are at a disadvantage. In addition to less earning power, compared with

---

80. Kearney, *Two-Parent Privilege*, 36.
81. Kramer, "US World's Highest Rate," paras. 2–3.
82. Statistics Canada, "Lone-Parent Families," table 2.
83. United States Census Bureau, "Census Bureau Releases," para. 2.

married couples, these families don't have the full-time parenting support of a second parent. In many cases, the other parent is absent in the life of the child. As we have shown previously, children in married-parent families tend to exhibit better behavioral, educational, and economic outcomes.

Most of us acknowledge that lone parenting is a difficult task. We are well versed in the financial struggles of single parents, particularly lone mothers. The data show overrepresentation of lone-parent families among low-income families. We should be no less acquainted with the other struggles, like having less time. Children are demanding and require much of their parents (demands that vary by age, of course). Thus lone parenting, beyond concerns about finances, can also be *lonely*—an emotional burden. One solo mom of a five-year-old recounts the simple difficulty of always being on duty and never getting a mental break: "I get one when we go visit my parents. But they live four hours from here, and we don't get there very often," she says. The simple reprieve of getting ten minutes to oneself is a luxury for solo parents.

How we consider lone-parent families in society, and in relationship to intact married parents, requires careful thought. A 2022 study from the Pew Research Center found that nearly half of Americans now say "single women raising children on their own is generally a bad thing for society."[84] In fact, the portion of Americans with this opinion has increased seven percentage points since 2018.[85] In one sense, this could indicate that many Americans recognize that lone-parent families (and, in the case of the Pew survey, that lone-mother-led families in particular) are disproportionately disadvantaged and that this has implications for society. It may also be an acknowledgment that many of these children are experiencing the absence of a parent. Others will interpret the result of the Pew data as evidence of growing stigma against lone-parent families. Programs and policies that support families in need are at risk when public sentiment stigmatizes the recipients.

---

84. Hurst, "Rising Share," para. 2.
85. Hurst, "Rising Share," para. 2.

Unfortunately, narratives that pit lone-parent families against intact, married-parent families are not uncommon. Canada's national newspaper, the *Globe and Mail*, ran a long story in 2024 about the financial challenges many lone-parent families face. The article asked, "How can governments escape the shadow of twentieth-century family values?"[86] The premise to the question was that public policy favors "nuclear families" to the disadvantage of lone parents. This assertion is certainly debatable. The article also fails to acknowledge something of a mini policy miracle. The rate of poverty among Canadian, female-headed, lone-parent families with at least one child aged zero to five decreased by more than half between 2015 and 2020.[87] Cash transfers such as the Canada Child Benefit likely contributed to this decrease. Still, this family form remains disproportionately represented among low-income Canadians.

There is no doubt that lone-parent families are more likely to experience hardship. Yet we can hold two views at the same time. We can strive to see children raised by both their parents in an intact married family, and we can do so without disparaging lone-parent families or withdrawing support.

One encouraging feature of lone-parenting life is the resourceful ways lone-parent families are building community and supporting one another. Many civil society groups, including religious organizations, have specific programs to support lone-parent families. We can recognize the stability of intact, married families without neglecting, stigmatizing, or devaluing the important parenting work of lone parents.

### Delayed Marriage

As we consider the pushing and pulling at marriage, there's one little data point that can tell us a lot about how we consider marriage in our own lives and the role marriage plays in culture and community: the age at which we get married. In the 1970s, the average

---

86. McGinn, "Single Parents Struggle," deck.
87. Statistics Canada, "Disaggregated Trends in Poverty," bullet point 5.

age of first marriage was twenty-two for women and twenty-four for men. Today we see the average age of first marriage hovering just above thirty for men and just below thirty for women in Canada and the United States.[88] Ultimately, getting married young signals the beginning of a life together. Earlier marriage, still today, serves as a foundation on which to grow assets, purchase property, have and parent children, and build a life.

Some call this the cornerstone view of marriage, meaning participants build their lives around that stone. University students today may be surprised to learn that not too long ago, there were on-campus dorms specifically for married couples. There were enough young people taking university classes who were married that there was a purpose to offering this space. Contrast with today, where married university students, if found at all, would more likely be completing a PhD than an undergraduate degree. I (Andrea) was shocked to meet not one but two married students in my postgraduate studies. Though these students were adults by any standard, I couldn't believe they were already married while still in school. Of course, the married-couple dorms were by then already long gone.

Today, getting married is more likely to occur once other milestones have already been achieved. It's almost as if partnership in marriage is seen as an impediment to achievement. Some call this the capstone view of marriage—it's the final stone placed on an already completed building. Couples today are more likely to complete schooling, develop careers, seek greater financial stability, purchase property, and even have children prior to getting married. Some of this delay is facilitated by cultural expectations; some comes from the absence of religious expectations; some is the result of the extended period of time it takes to become adults; and some is due to more reliable forms of birth control, like oral contraception, and the breaking of the connection between sex and marriage. Often a combination of factors are at play. Ultimately, delayed marriage is not due to one simple factor.

---

88. Cardus, "Canadian Marriage Map"; United States Census Bureau, *Median Age*.

The capstone view of marriage reflects how few people prioritize matrimony. Yet we shouldn't assume that the rising age at first marriage is purely the result of personal choice for all.

Marriage as a destination on the road map of life is not always chosen consciously or intentionally. For example, an expensive degree entails paying back the student loan by working hard for several years. Once on the path of needing to get out of debt, it may mean deferring marriage until financial stability is achieved. Another factor is that men and boys aren't doing as well these days,[89] but women still prefer to marry men who earn more than they do.[90] We haven't begun to mention the decline of dating culture and how difficult it is to start modern relationships; it's more difficult to find a mate in a culture that undervalues the permanency of marriage, resulting in many years of searching. So, more often than not, delayed marriage may be something we slide into rather than the result of choices freely made.[91] Many spend years and even decades searching for the right partner to marry; delayed marriage was not their first choice. Sadly, for those who desire marriage, the rising age at first marriage means that larger numbers of people will not get married at all.

If marriage is viewed as a destination rather than a starting point, it will remain out of reach for some who desire it. This is particularly true with regard to economic factors such as rising inflation. It's extremely hard for many younger people, particularly in Canada, to consider purchasing a home, for example. If this is seen as a prerequisite to getting married and/or having children, some people, particularly in the lower-income brackets, are simply never going to get there. This is indeed borne out by

89. Reeves, *Of Boys and Men*.
90. Institute for Family Studies, "Better-Educated Women."
91. "Sliding" versus "deciding" is a phrase coined by marriage scholar Scott Stanley and his colleagues to describe how many couples start living together. A toothbrush moves over to the other's house, then a garment or two, and so on. Several months later, a couple may be living together without ever having had a conversation about their relational aspirations (Stanley et al., "Sliding versus Deciding"). Marriage, on the other hand, requires intentionality. We cannot assume marriage will forever be there along with its social goods if we consistently take it for granted.

marriage statistics both north and south of the border—that marriage is more or less intact in the upper classes but has broken down among lower classes.[92]

## Approaching Marriage as a Contract

In 2011, a legislator in Mexico City proposed the short-term marriage contract. No more would "till death do us part" reign. The proposal was for marriages to be reevaluated every two years.[93] This was more of an attempt to curtail the destruction of legal divorce battles than to erode the institution of marriage. Still, nothing quite takes the wind out of marriage sails like attempting to preemptively address the fact that some marriages, even a large percentage, will end in divorce, by effectively obligating divorce and remarriage on two-year intervals. The periodic essays explaining that "forever" marriages are a relic of an era when lifespans were shorter and economic well-being was tied to marriage only add fuel to the fire. Thus, we see proposals for a new model of renewable marriages that would allow partners to dissolve the relationship and move on after a set number of years.[94]

At the heart of these proposals is the notion that marriage is contractual and that term limits would protect the interests of both signatories to the contract. If the current relationship does not meet your needs or prevents you from developing your full potential, simply choose not to renew the contract and move on.

While marriage has legal, contractual obligations, it is not best described as a contractual relationship. We may ask whether pushing it ever more into the domain of contracts detracts from the bigger picture of the role that marriage is intended to fill. As we have emphasized, the permanency of marriage is one of the stabilizing elements of the institution. Even as partners mature and grow, institutional marriage allows them to shift and accommodate one another as they continue to build their marriage.

   92. Hymowitz, *Marriage and Caste*; Mitchell and Cross, "Marriage Gap."
   93. Romo, "Mexican Legislator."
   94. Larson, "Renewable Marriage Contracts."

Contracts in other domains clearly itemize specific commitments and timelines. Consider that a contract with a house painter specifies the date the painter will come, the list of rooms to be painted, itemized repairs required in order to paint, and of course the cost. If we tried to write up all the commitments of marriage into a contract, lawyers would soon find themselves overwhelmed. All too often there are obligations that simply cannot be foreseen. This is another way of helping us to understand marriage as an institution. Institutions serve as a bundle of formal and informal rules, social norms, legal and natural rights, and obligations that constrain behaviors and guide interactions in order to achieve desired outcomes in a way that legal contracts cannot.[95] Economist Jennifer Roback Morse, formerly of Yale University, writes, "The presumption of contract is that the parties are making an explicit exchange of promises for fairly well-defined objects or services and within a clearly delineated time frame."[96] Roback Morse argues that the contract understanding of marriage is insufficient in capturing the scope of a lifetime relationship in which commitments and duties shift throughout the life course.

Marriage cannot be like this. There is not a contract in the world that can delineate all the responsibilities spouses will encounter over the course of their lives. Hence an institutional approach to marriage rests on marriage itself as providing the frame to hold love as the feelings ebb and flow over time, in specific situations, with specific difficulties, obligations, and joys.

Institutional marriage anticipates that there will be trade-offs and sacrifices made for the other partner that will have future benefits for both couples. Consider, for example, when one partner exits the workforce to acquire more schooling or training for the benefit of future family income. Rather than being constrictive, the permanence of marriage allows for greater creativity and opportunity.

---

95. For more on what institutions do in society, see Allen, *Institutional Revolution*.

96. Morse, *Love and Economics*, 76.

# 4

# Living an Ancient Institution in Modern Times

MARRIAGE IS A HUMAN universal, present throughout recorded history.[1] We don't often linger on this point, but marriage is, in fact, ancient. There are few ceremonies, traditions, or aspects of our common lives today that tap into such a deep history. Perhaps this is part of the conundrum for marriage today. On the one hand, this longevity makes the marriage proposition attractive. In a transient world, a microwave culture, a culture saturated with self-image, and a fixation with the here and now, the ability to tap into the ancient roots of an other-focused institution like marriage is an unusual gift. On the other hand, this is why marriage presents difficulties for our modern minds, leaving us asking ourselves whether we still need it. Many of the historical realities that made marriage an unquestionable social need either are, or feel as though they are, less pressing today—things like protection of children over the life course or protection of mothers in childbirth.

So how old is marriage? It was Aristotle, living about three hundred years before Christ, who suggested that marriage is "an older and more fundamental thing than the state," which grew out

---

1. Coontz, *Marriage, a History*, 24.

of love between a man and a woman.[2] For Aristotle, the stability of any state depended on the success of households founded on "the natural procreative union of male and female."[3] In this early understanding, marriage is essential to household stability, and household stability is essential to the success of the polity. This also speaks to the idea that marriage is not a government creation. Rather, it precedes the state, and where marriages are healthy, and thus families stable, it contributes to a government's success. Samantha, age forty-six, made the same point without citing Aristotle: "Marriage is a microclimate, a microcosm of society as a whole. If the cells are healthy, the body is healthy. Marriage is the canary in the coal mine concerning the health of the culture."

More recently, the great thinkers of the Enlightenment did not make marriage and family a focal point. If marriage is a human universal, found across time and cultures, it is not hard to imagine why it would have flown below the radar as a subject of study. The philosopher Thomas Hobbes, best known for his view that without a well-functioning state, people's lives would be "nasty, brutish, and short," believed people needed a monarch to rule over civilized existence because civilization was fragile.[4] For Hobbes, marriage was a part of civilized existence—a part of the transition from "the state of nature to society, from barbarism to civilization."[5] It was also only with the development of "matrimonial laws," he said, that fathers would join in on the child-rearing proposition.[6]

The philosopher John Locke, too, spoke of the bond between man and wife as "the first society," calling this bond the seedbed of all human society. Families, thought Locke, "are rooted in biological facts, and marriage is a contrivance arising to deal with those

---

2. Aristotle, *Ethics*, as cited in Blankenhorn, *Future of Marriage*, 23.

3. Brake, "Marriage and Domestic Partnership," sect. 2., "Understanding Marriage: Historical Orientation," para. 3.

4. Blankenhorn, *Future of Marriage*, 25.

5. Blankenhorn, *Future of Marriage*, 26.

6. Blankenhorn, *Future of Marriage*, 25.

facts." In Locke's view, "marriages and families are artificial institutions designed to answer the natural needs of children."[7]

Stable families, based in marriage, help engender civilized, democratic public cultures, Locke thought. He writes this: "Without such nursing Fathers tender and carefull of the publick weale, all governments would have sunk under the Weakness and Infirmities of their Infancy."[8] Marriage acted then, as it acts now, to moderate behavior toward the good of the other. The American public intellectual Mary Eberstadt, writing about contemporary culture, argues that "snowflake" millennials are actually sensitive with very good reason.[9] They are less likely to have had the benefits of a stable, secure upbringing. Many young people today are plagued by some of the insecurities and wounds "of their Infancy."

Both Hobbes and Locke were reckoning with an advancement of individual rights as well, which some academics argue created problems for marriage. "In the early modern era, as doctrines of equal rights and contract appeared, a new ideal of relationships between adults as free choices between equals appeared. In this light, the unequal and unchosen content of the marriage relationship raised philosophical problems," writes marriage scholar Elizabeth Brake.[10] We are likely living out some of these philosophical problems today. It's not that individual rights necessarily run contrary to a society that values marriage and family but rather that our current conception of what constitutes individual rights has been stretched into a form of hyper-individualism. Today, voluntarily constraining individual liberty within a marriage in order to achieve a joint benefit may feel like too much sacrifice for some.

Jonah Goldberg, author of *Suicide of the West*, describes marriage as marking progress out of chaos. In his own Hobbesian moment he identifies "poverty, hunger, violence, tribal hatred, and an early death" as our early natural state. Monogamous

---

7. Yenor, *Family Politics*, 21.
8. Yenor, *Family Politics*, 22.
9. M. Eberstadt, *Primal Screams*.
10. Brake, "Marriage and Domestic Partnership," sect. 2., "Understanding Marriage: Historical Orientation," para. 7.

marriage may not be natural, then, but it does represent an advancement from some of the harshness that was once a normal part of the human condition. He does not ask whether marriage is natural or unnatural, or what definition is "the best," but rather, what works. He concludes, "We made traditional marriage normal through centuries of civilizational trial and error because countless generations of wise people figured out that it was a best practice for society." The family's fight against barbarism, he says, is grounded, if not in marriage, then at the very least in lasting monogamous relationships.[11] We might add that marriage protects monogamy, and a lasting monogamous relationship is exactly what marriage is intended to be. More and more research, which we explored in chapter 2, explains how and why children raised by their own married parents fare better on a number of different factors—staying out of criminal behavior, for example. These factors point to an assumed basis for living in a calm, peaceful—civilized and socialized—world.

Living an ancient institution in modern times means more than accruing benefits like increased wealth or improved health. The stability of marriage could be an attractive transcendent proposition for those individuals who feel unmoored or cast adrift in a transient world. Marriage is a complex institution because it has evolved with input from diverse groups over time. Yet this ancient institution remains at the core of our lives because it works. We have argued that no one should feel compelled to marry but that a critical mass of intact married families is still good for the health of communities. As marriage rates decline, our culture has lost the language and logic of the ancient institution. The rising prominence of the soulmate model of marriage reflects our culture's highly individualistic approach to partnership, one that centers on the needs and desires of the individual.

So now we ask: How can we rebuild a healthy marriage culture? Can this ancient institution be reimagined as ever relevant and necessary in contemporary culture?

11. Goldberg, *Suicide of the West*, 266.

## Telling a Better Story

We've already mentioned that we shouldn't look for marriage stories in the rom-com or Disney fairy tale section; rather, marriage is more like a Tolkien-style adventure. Happy-clappy, romanticized versions of marriage are proving to be inadequate in the face of the inevitable challenges and hardships couples face. Marriage is not happily ever after but involves sacrifice and hardship alongside joy and companionship. We need to be realistic about the highs and lows, and the commitment necessary to endure.

It may seem odd that, as part of our "telling a better story" section, we start by referencing lows and endurance. This is a starting point, however, because it recognizes the reality and the normal experiences that happen over the life course of every marriage. Further, because many adults and children have been hurt, speaking openly of these realities allows for greater possibilities to heal. This also allows us to own the ways in which we have not supported marriage. There's no perfect person, and there are no perfect relationships. Allowing for this as a starting point means we can truly point to the adventure and not the romance of marriage. "Here be dragons" is a better leitmotif for telling a better story about marriage than "you complete me."

In addition to recognizing the highs and lows and the personal losses from the divorce revolution, we must acknowledge the loss experienced by individuals and families when marriage disappears from whole communities. As noted earlier, marriage has declined more rapidly among North Americans with lower educational attainment and lower income. Efforts to revitalize a healthy marriage culture must recognize that for many people, marriage seems out of reach because nowhere is it currently present as an example. Telling a better story means finding people to tell the story of marriage to those communities with a voice that will be heard, people with street cred who can enter into a community and come alongside without preaching from on high. Who tells the story is as important as the story itself, and not every storyteller will suit every audience.

Finally, rebuilding a healthy marriage culture will be slow work. Rather than harking back to a fictional golden age, rebuilding the ancient institution will require attentiveness to new realities without losing the logic of what makes marriage work.

## Modeling Marriage

Telling a story is one side of the equation. But healthy marriage is caught as much as taught. It needs to be modeled in order to thrive. Modeling marriage does not mean pretending to attain the perfect marriage. There is no shame in having a mediocre marriage—the marriage that shows up, without fireworks, every day. There are high points and low points, "in sickness and in health," and the world is better off for them. It does not take a perfect marriage (since there is no such thing) to be counted as a role model. Modeling healthy marriage is work every married couple can do, with or without children, in our workplaces and in our communities.

While modeling healthy marriage need not be a formalized program, the institutions of civil society, such as places of worship, are well positioned to support this work. For example, the Catholic Diocese of Montreal has recently incorporated a mentorship model into its premarital counseling. Innovative programs like Marital First Responders equip adults to navigate conversations with friends and family who are struggling in their marriages. The program is a great example of how individuals play a supportive role in building a healthy marriage culture. The program helps people confidently support their friends and family.

Deliberately providing realistic examples of how to be married doesn't mean rushing young people to the altar, but we can certainly provide young adults with a better sense of purpose for marriage and how one may direct their life toward such a goal.

## Giving Young Adults the Goods

No, not everyone is meant to marry, but the reality is that many are well suited for married life but are uncertain about the path toward establishing a healthy, stable family.

With the loss of the language and logic of marriage, learning about healthy marriage must begin long before young adults consider tying the knot. Marriage may not be seen as necessary, an attitude we hope to have a small part in changing, but that doesn't mean it's not wanted. One challenge is that we do not offer young adults a clear path to achieve the family life many desire. We counsel young adults toward academic and career pathways, but we give little direction regarding how to pursue a healthy family life. Jennifer, age twenty-four, told us, "I can recognize my understanding of marriage has been shaped by my environment and am in the process of delineating what marriage can and should be." Why should Jennifer be left to figure it out on her own? Extended family and education establishments can both play a role.

As marriage rates have been declining, it's time to begin communicating the advantages and benefits of marriage for individuals and society. Our cultural and political leaders need to sing from the same songbook about the benefits of stable families and the purpose of marriage. In our experience, this public expression is more likely to be found in the United States and the United Kingdom, where public intellectuals are less reluctant than in Canada to discuss the role of marriage in our common lives today. Conversations around poverty and inequality in the United States occasionally debate the role of marriage and family structure, but such debates are comparatively absent in Canada.

School-based curricula could address the benefits of marriage and the success sequence described earlier. Relationship education across the continent tends to focus on sex but to shy away from providing guidance on or even mentioning healthy marriage. So many sex-ed curricula offer no clear pathway toward lifelong partnerships. This is a disservice to young people. As we have already shown, schools should teach students about the success sequence, an ordering of life events that has been shown to dramatically lower the risk of poverty.

School curricula can be a secondary source of information. Civil society institutions that serve youth and young adults have an important role. But most importantly, families need to be empowered to see their own place as the first teachers, showing the way toward healthy relationships.

### Culture, Law, and the Role of the State

Having worked in family policy for nearly two decades, it's tempting to approach family issues by thinking first about what governments can do. However, our public policy experience tempers our expectations. Family policy experts Richard Reeves and Christopher Pulliam caution, "When it comes to some of the most intimate decisions in a person's life—how and when to form a family—it is important to be humble about the limits of public policy."[12]

When we contemplate the role of the state, it is helpful to consider the interest the state has in family life and the limits to actions it should undertake. Families provide love and care in ways the state can't duplicate. Acknowledging this fact, however, does not mean denying there are ways in which the state can help families.

Growing families are a benefit to the state. The state has an interest in stable families, particularly when children are involved. Safe, stable, and nurturing homes contribute to the development of a healthy citizenry. With declining fertility rates and aging populations, the social safety net will face significant strain in the future. Growing families develop networks within communities and connect with other civil society institutions. These bonds contribute to the development of social capital and enhance well-being. Most children in North America are born to married parents. The intact, married-parent family remains an important institution in strengthening communities. Thus, a

---

12. Reeves and Pulliam, "Middle Class Marriage Declining," "What Can Be Done," para. 1.

significant factor in the state's interest in marriage is the well-being of children. But families, not the state, are the primary institution responsible for child well-being.

Some people argue that the state should get out of the marriage license business. It certainly would be possible to stop licensing marriages, but the state would still be involved when families dissolve. At the time of this writing, the province of Quebec has introduced a bill to create a new legal category called "parental union." Remember, Quebec is a place with some of the lowest marriage rates in the world. It has, in some sense, gotten the state out of the marriage business, since so few Quebeckers choose marriage. Under the legislation, unmarried couples would become a parental union when they have a child together. The bill outlines which assets are divisible when a parental union dissolves.[13] With 67 percent of births in Quebec occurring outside a married-parent union in 2022, the province has had to create a legal structure that protects partners and children in the event of a breakup.[14] What this points to is the necessity of state involvement if not in marriage, then in dissolution, especially as concerns children. Even in the absence of a marriage culture, the state has had to create a category of partnerships to protect children at the point of dissolution.

For as long as the state issues marriage licenses, it will need to define marriage and articulate a rationale for which partnerships constitute a marriage. Many companionate relationships, such as deep and meaningful friendships, provide people with meaning and well-being but don't constitute marriage. That doesn't mean these other companionate relationships are less important in our lives. But marriage is a particular relationship that is exclusionary by design. (For example, it excludes minors and multiple partners.) The state needs to have a clear rationale concerning how it defines marriage and where and why it asserts itself in this domain.

As we have noted throughout this book, the decline of marriage has been particularly evident among socioeconomically

---

13. CBC, "Quebec Tables Bill."

14. Calculations by authors from Statistics Canada, "Live Births," under "Quebec, Place of Residence of Mother."

disadvantaged North Americans. Thus, especially for these communities, the state can play a role in removing some of the barriers to forming married families. One example is the removal of marriage penalties within government programs. Some assistance programs aimed at low-income adults can unintentionally dissuade the recipient from marrying because they would see a significant clawback in benefits. For example, I (Peter Jon) know a couple who postponed getting married for years because the marriage would have resulted in a dramatic financial reduction of disability benefits.

The state, we have argued, is not the primary actor in developing a healthy marriage culture, but it should not be disinterested. When families dissolve, the state often has to step in. It is not well positioned to care for children when families neglect or are unable to fulfill their primary responsibilities. Political leaders and policymakers could be more engaged in speaking about the importance of this ancient institution in modern life.

### Promoting the Beauty of Marriage

This book is ultimately an effort, using social-scientific research, to initiate a conversation about reimagining what marriage is and why it still matters. But alongside that ethos, we also are people who are cheerleading the concept of healthy marriages. Empowering others to do the same means preaching it, to some extent, in a way that is motivating for others to catch the vision. In that sense, some will model marriage, some will speak about it, some will research it, some will promote it. There are scholars who add significant caveats to the benefits of marriage but ultimately contend that the philosophy or worldview of the sexual revolution is less successful than a stable, lifelong marriage and less likely to bring about meaning in a person's life. We need to name this reality in the face of opposition. The bottom line is that we can no longer take marriage for granted. Public conversations about the benefits of marriage and the role family structure plays in well-being equip people with the knowledge to make their own informed choices and help public policymakers identify barriers to family formation.

# 5

# Reflections on Our Work

### Candice Malcolm

> *Candice Malcolm is a bestselling author, investigative journalist, nationally syndicated columnist with the Toronto Sun, and the founder and editor-in-chief of True North. She has reported from war zones, broken news stories that have made headlines worldwide, and exposed major terrorist networks operating in Canada. Born and raised in Vancouver, British Columbia, Candice has two master's degrees, has traveled all over the world, and is married with four little kids.*

MY LIFE CHANGED—IN AN earth-shattering way—when I was ten years old. My parents called a family meeting where they calmly announced to their five young children that they were getting a divorce. I never saw it coming. I'd never heard my parents so much as raise their voices toward one another.

I had thought we were a happy and thriving family. My young brain couldn't comprehend what it meant, and what it would mean for my family and me going forward.

I . . . DO?

Everything about my life changed after that. Everything that I thought was routine and safe and secure and normal was suddenly gone. My entire world was shattered, and the next decade of my life felt like a roller coaster of unwanted change.

I sort of chuckle when I hear people on the political left talk about "privilege"—of which I'm sure I have plenty. But by the time I grew into adulthood, I saw only one type of privilege: two-parent-household privilege.

Growing up in a stable, predictable environment with a mother and a father working together, utilizing their biological strengths to provide everything a child could need, is something that cannot be matched—no matter your skin color, your last name, or how rich your parents are. I'm fortunate in that many of my close friends came from stable, intact, secure families. I could see what they had, which made it harder and sadder for me that I didn't have it too.

So how does that make me fortunate? Well, because I didn't become cynical about marriage. I didn't become one of those "it's just a piece of paper" types. I saw my friends' families up close, and I cherished what they had—a mother and a father, in a covenant, working together and devoted to their family.

This was particularly my experience as a student at the University of Alberta in Edmonton as part of a tight-knit sorority on campus. I got plenty of invites to family dinners and holiday celebrations, and I was able to see firsthand the incredible family bonds that exist on the prairies (often in intergenerational Catholic homes).

I learned the importance and value of marriage by growing up in a broken one.

I'm not saying I had bad parents. The opposite is true—I have truly wonderful and loving parents, who made the most of a bad situation and worked incredibly hard to make sure I didn't fall off my path. They gave me everything I could ever want, and I remain incredibly close with both of them. (In fact, my mother moved in with us during COVID to help with our young kids and is part of the reason I can be both a stay-at-home mom and the editor-in-chief of *True North*.)

By the time I finished school and started dating seriously, I had developed incredibly strong feelings about marriage.

I met my husband in my mid-twenties (we were both political staffers who had recently been transported to Ottawa), and on our first date, I kid you not, I told him that I don't date for "fun"—I date for marriage, and I don't believe in divorce.

I'm sure many men in that age group in today's culture would run for the hills if a woman said something like that, but fortunately again, my husband agreed. Strongly. Turns out we were kindred millennial souls, traditionalists trying to navigate a broken, liberal, feminist world.

We got married a few years later (and recently celebrated our ten-year anniversary!).

Everything about my life got exponentially better after being married. I instantly felt that stability I'd been longing for since childhood. I had someone who wasn't going anywhere. Someone who loved me, supported me, cherished me, helped me, and centered me.

And in return, I would do anything for my husband, to support and encourage him on his incredible journey. And I have! We've taken huge risks together: we've moved and have now lived in three countries, we've started several businesses each (some have failed spectacularly, others have been wildly successful), and, most importantly, we have four beautiful children together.

While our secular, liberal, feminist culture told me that the key to living a happy and productive life was to embrace a career path, become financially independent, loathe or pity men, treat them as disposable, engage in random and casual hookup culture, and put myself above everything else, that always seemed flat-out wrong to me.

Even as a product of a broken marriage (which is so much harder than our culture acknowledges) and coming from the secular, liberal, feminist corner of society, I still gravitated toward the institution.

Marriage has worked for millennia, and feminism is failing us after a few short decades. Sadly for my generation and those that follow, we were the guinea pigs of a culture that said "lean in" and "have it all!" The *Sex and the City* gals were held up as the ultimate icons of fashion and culture, never mind the fact that the characters were based on gay men and the creator is now a sad, lonely, sixty-something woman who gives interviews about how she wishes she had gotten married and had children.

The outcome of feminism is playing out before our eyes. We see a generation of young men and women who don't seem compatible, who have diverging values and political views, who are dating less and having less sex, who seem angry and bitter with the opposite sex—in short, a generation of young adults who are not worthy of marriage and in turn don't see marriage as worthwhile.

Changing this trajectory, encouraging marriage as a social good, and, most importantly, encouraging everyone to have more kids is a generational imperative that will take years if not decades to advance.

But it's my firm belief that it is the most important issue facing our country and our society. The right solutions are the ones outlined in this book. We should not water down or change marriage to make it more palatable in our lost world. We need to make the case for traditional marriage, to remind young people of the purpose of traditions and how they form the foundation of our society.

Part of growing up is learning to become worthy of marriage, to think about what you can offer in a marriage (rather than just what you want from marriage or what you're looking for in a partner), and to embrace your life's journey.

As hedonism becomes mainstream, more and more people will look to tradition to find purpose and meaning in the world, and I'm pleased this book is here as a resource. Read it and buy it for your kids or your friends or whomever may need a gentle reminder that families must remain the central institution in our society—otherwise, governments will happily fill that void.

## Lyman Stone

> Lyman Stone is a demographer specializing in fertility and family. He is also the director of research for the demographic consulting firm Demographic Intelligence, senior fellow at the Institute for Family Studies' Pronatalism Initiative, and a PhD candidate in sociology at McGill University. He, his wife, and their three daughters live in Kentucky.

There was audible giggling when my wife and I exchanged our vows; we almost laughed at ourselves as we said, "I plight thee my troth." Some friends thought we'd done some faux-antique kind of individualized vows. But no, we were simply using the same exact service that others had used before us in that church since they first switched from German to English, and that English translation itself was inspired by older English-language wording for a wedding. Our choice to use an old service design was intentional, and it was, in a sociologically important sense, extremely individualistic of us: we were asserting our own unique flavor over and against a mainstream culture in which "troth plighting" is not the usual vocabulary of marriage. In our ceremony, then, was a bizarre fact: we were on the one hand making an overt appeal to a community-held tradition pulled out of the well of history from a *far* less individualistic time . . . and yet in making this conscious and distinctive choice, we were also setting ourselves apart as culturally distinct individuals vis-à-vis our wider society. We were being individualistic in eschewing individualism.

This book has laid out a lot of important facts about marriage, which boil down to: it is mostly a pretty good thing, it would be nice if we had a bit more of it, and yet people don't think all that highly of it, and so society should at various levels perhaps promote marriage a bit more. On all these fronts I can only say: quite so!

But the case of Quebec really demands that we confront the problem of individualism head-on. Mrozek and Mitchell do address Quebec directly, but mostly to suggest (I think rightly) that it is not a template for other places. Nonetheless, it is a case from which we can learn, as it can help us to get a better idea of what this "individualism" thing is that has been so influential in modern societies and had such a big effect on marriage. Explaining Quebec's history to friends who visited my wife and me in Montreal, I would summarize by saying, "In Quebec, the Reformation came four hundred years late—and instead of Protestantism, the successor ideology was secular Québécois nationalism." That ideology was, apparently, individualistic in the extreme—the hospitals where my wife bore two of our children refused to call her by her legal last name because it was also *my* last name, and the papers for our children called them "Ruth's baby." Not Ruth *and Lyman's* baby: Ruth's.

But of course, in another sense, this new ideology was not very individualistic at all. Quebec's distinct society is welfarist, offering much more generous social supports than is typical in Canada. When we lived in Montreal, we got all sorts of benefits thanks to having kids, and we enjoyed an extensive range of public and municipal services: now back in America, no such luck. Moreover, while perhaps refusing to take a husband's surname was a bold assertion of individualism in 1965, it is no longer. Since 1981 Quebec law requires women (and men) in Quebec to use their birth name in all legal and state-related contexts (although they can choose to use their spouse's name in social settings if they wish). In some societies, observing that a couple has different surnames really tells you something *about that couple*, about their views of marriage, their identity. In Quebec, that isn't so: non-shared surnames are now the norm. What was once a hallmark of individualism is now a legal requirement. If what we mean by *individualism* is "a set of social norms establishing that individuals should emphasize and signal their differences and unique attributes to others," then it isn't clear to me that Quebec is a very individualist place at all. It's just that the locus of social control changed from the Catholic Church to the state or, arguably, to whichever set of intellectuals and influencers happen to be able to steer cultural opinion for a generation or so.

Only a nonconformist individual in Quebec would, say, not cohabit before marriage or get married in a religious ceremony. That life course is highly unusual—statistically, it's probably fewer than 10 percent of women in Quebec. Women breaking from the norm in Quebec are likely complying with a norm in their country of origin. Probably almost everybody in Quebec is basically just doing the normal thing—coupling the way Québécois people are *supposed* to couple—that is, with low commitment, periodic cohabitation, marriage only after a long time if ever, without a shared surname, and usually without a religious ceremony.

I think individualism has been a sort of convenient talking point for a long time because it has a pleasant kind of neutrality to it; it doesn't immediately code in a specific political way. But I think this is a misreading of the social terrain around marriage. In Quebec, marriage declined because revolutionary elites self-consciously believed and quite publicly said (and legislated accordingly) that Catholic marriage norms were bad, and that a different set of more sexually permissive norms, which publicly downgraded the degree of sharing in married unions, was much better. This change is not well described as individualistic or not. It's not as if Quebec just changed its laws to say, actually, you can take your husband's surname or not, your choice. And while Quebec is an outlier, the truth is that the story in other areas of North America is not so different: society, led by influential opinion makers, didn't suddenly fall more in love with freedom; it just downgraded its view of marriage.

I am a loud American and so tend to lack the tact and subtlety of my more judicious northern neighbors. Marriage has not declined because of some nebulous individualism, some newfound freedom. Marriage has declined because governments and influential figures in civil society decided to reduce the economic and social benefits accruing to marriage, and this decision arose from a belief that marriage was not quite as good a thing as had been claimed, and perhaps was quite a bad thing (for women, at least). For quite a few decades, a lot of policies have basically been designed in such a way that they can be expected to reduce marriage rates, and a lot of the political willingness to permit this design arose from a straightforward belief, not in *individualism* but rather in the idea that marriage wasn't very good. This belief, among political decision-makers and opinion shapers, essentially resulted in norms and policies that made anti-marriage decisions *for* individuals, structuring their lives so that marriage was disadvantageous regardless of their own individual desires. It wasn't individualism; it was the same old social control but directed to a new end.

We do, as Mrozek and Mitchell note, need to tell a new story. But this story will probably depend, for its success, on an enormous amount of individualism. Aggressively nonconformist individuals and minority communities will have to deviate from conformity with prevailing anti-marriage social norms and send strong signals of their individual-level uniqueness by, say, sharing a last name, or refusing to cohabit, or having five kids, and so on. One piece of evidence that the future of "traditional" things like marriage and big families actually lies in *more* individualism rather than *less* can be found in baby names: in the United States at least, biblical baby names are in decline . . . unless they are *weird* biblical baby names. "David" and "John" are vanishing, but "Obadiah" or "Asa"? Those names are filling the kindergarten classrooms. Increasingly, religious parents manifest their religiosity by picking ever more unusual and obscure Bible names for their kids, leaning into their traditional values while also signaling extremely high social nonconformism and individualism. Thus, where Mrozek and Mitchell identify the project facing marriage advocates as a kind of recovery of older things, the most likely path forward for marriage advocates may be quite different: not a return to past traditions, but going through the looking glass, into a world of even more radical individualism. In this world, young people enter into something like traditional marriage not because it is traditional, but because they can find a version of that tradition that is so different from the mainstream that it is a useful signal of individualistic traits and values.

# Conclusion

In G. K. Chesterton's "fence parable," a person comes upon a fence spanning a road and declares it "useless." Chesterton wrote, "The more modern type of reformer goes gaily up to it and says, 'I don't see the use of this; let us clear it away.' To which the more intelligent type of reformer will do well to answer: 'If you don't see the use of it, I certainly won't let you clear it away. Go away and think. Then, when you can come back and tell me that you do see the use of it, I may allow you to destroy it.'"[1] We have argued that many North Americans find marriage nice but unnecessary, one option among many choices for young adults who are growing more and more uninterested in the institution.

Like Chesterton's fence, we are concerned that too many people come upon marriage and say something like, "I see no use of this." They may not follow by saying, "Let us clear it away"; rather, they may step in with something of a "you do you" mentality. But the lack of interest and engagement in the larger question of "why marriage" risks a society where we do in fact push the marriage fence down or abandon it to rot and decay. How many policies do we choose without regard for maintaining the strengths of marriage? Which cultural norms have evolved that do not support marriage? How do policy and culture partner together to detract from marital strengths? How many young people no longer

---

1. Chesterton, "Drift from Domesticity," 53.

practice a faith that supports marriage? How many faiths fail to practically support or promote marriage?

There are many ways to risk losing marriage. It's not that there has been an intention to eradicate a fence across a road (marriage), but rather that in many little ways we've forgotten that even important, long-standing institutions can crumble if left untended. Either the institution crumbles, or we ourselves no longer understand how to incorporate it into our lives. Social institutions evolve, of course, but there must remain a core function and a shared understanding of marriage in our private lives and in our communities. And for this to remain, we need to advocate for marriage, point to the goods it produces, and inform ourselves.

Marriage still matters. It is essential, and it not only offers a path toward a privately fulfilling life but also builds into community strengths. We've argued that marriage is more than an outward symbol of a private commitment or loving relationship. It is a social institution that bundles formal and informal rules, social norms, legal and natural rights, and obligations that partners freely enter. Marriage requires voluntarily constraining behaviors in order to produce desired outcomes. We've presented some of the evidence showing that, on the whole, a healthy marriage is correlated with positive outcomes for children, adults, and wider community.

To some readers, the value of marriage seems incontrovertible, like motherhood and apple pie. To others, marriage is irrelevant and passé, and society should move on. Our goal is to nurture an open-minded conversation filled with the sorts of questions that spur on an imagination of what marriage fully is. These questions will vary for each person and are influenced by our own experiences with family life. Imagining that marriage matters requires a good deal of thought, reading, and conversation. After all, even for the authors of this book, there remain questions. There is always even more to distill and consider. Importantly, in nurturing this open-ended discussion, we need not expect agreement but rather come to a point of disagreeing in goodwill—disagreeing about the real issues and not perceived ones.

## CONCLUSION

As we've said several times, no one needs to get married. We believe North Americans should appreciate the function of marriage in society, even if they determine the family form is not for them. Good-faith disagreement reflects engagement, and that's good for public discourse. As Canadians, we can't help but notice that scholars and public intellectuals in the United States and United Kingdom have debated the relevancy of marriage in the pages of popular publications and books in a way we have not witnessed in Canada. We hope to promote a public conversation in our own home country.

Despite the decline in marriage over the last number of decades, we are hopeful about the future of marriage. Reimagining a healthy marriage culture is not a matter of electing the right people into power or enacting the right combination of policies—though we have presented some policy directions. Marriage should not be a polarizing, politicized issue. While public policy certainly has its place in removing barriers to stable family life, it is communities and social institutions that play a key role in reimagining the future of marriage and strengthening individual marriages.

All this, of course, begins with understanding what marriage is and why we still have this social institution even today. It begins with reflection and conversation—a task to which we hope this book contributes.

# Bibliography

Adshade, Marina. "Does Marriage Really Make Us Healthier and Happier?" *Institute for Family Studies*, Nov. 6, 2019. https://ifstudies.org/blog/does-marriage-really-make-us-healthier-and-happier.

Aizer, Ayal A., et al. "Marital Status and Survival in Patients with Cancer." *Journal of Clinical Oncology* 31 (2013) 3869–76. https://doi.org/10.1200/JCO.2013.49.6489.

Allen, Douglas W. "The Anatomy of Canada's Child Support Guidelines: The Effects, Details, and History of a Feminist Family Policy." In *Research Handbook on the Economics of Family Law*, edited by Lloyd R. Cohen and Joshua D. Wright, 132–58. Cheltenham, UK: Elgar, 2011.

———. *The Institutional Revolution: Measurement and the Economic Emergence of the Modern World*. Markets and Governments in Economic History. Chicago: University of Chicago Press, 2011.

Alviar, Carlos, et al. "Association of Marital Status with Vascular Disease in Different Arterial Territories: A Population Based Study of over 3.5 Million Subjects." Supplement, *Journal of the American College of Cardiology* 63 (2014) A1328. https://doi.org/10.1016/S0735-1097(14)61328-0.

Amato, Paul. "Marriage, Cohabitation and Mental Health." *Family Matters* 96 (2015) 5–13. https://aifs.gov.au/publications/family-matters/issue-96/marriage-cohabitation-and-mental-health.

Anglin, Howard. "Country, Province, and Nation: Canada Is Not a Nation." *Hub*, Oct. 26, 2022. https://thehub.ca/2022/10/26/howard-anglin-country-province-and-nation-canada-is-not-a-nation.

Angus Reid Institute. "'I Don't: Four-in-Ten Canadian Adults Have Never Married, and Aren't Sure They Want To." *Angus Reid Institute*, May 7, 2018. http://angusreid.org/marriage-trends-canada.

Bachiochi, Erika. *The Rights of Women: Reclaiming a Lost Vision*. Catholic Ideas for a Secular World. Notre Dame, IN: University of Notre Dame Press, 2021.

# BIBLIOGRAPHY

Barzel, Yoram, and Douglas W. Allen. *Economic Analysis of Property Rights.* 3rd ed. Political Economy of Institutions and Decisions. Cambridge: Cambridge University Press, 2023.

Beaujot, Roderic, et al. "Family Policies in Quebec and the Rest of Canada: Implications for Fertility, Child-Care, Women's Paid Work, and Child Development Indicators." *Canadian Public Policy* 39 (2013) 221–40. https://doi.org/10.3138/CPP.39.2.221.

Beauvoir, Simone de. *The Second Sex.* New York: Knopf, 1953.

Benson, Harry. "Hopelessly Unhappy? Drifting Apart? Before You Give Up Hope for Your Marriage, Read This." *Mercator,* Feb. 5, 2024. https://www.mercatornet.com/unhappy_marriage_read_this.

———. "Why the Act of Marriage (Still) Makes a Difference." *Institute for Family Studies,* Mar. 16, 2022. https://ifstudies.org/blog/why-the-act-of-marriage-still-makes-a-difference.

Blankenhorn, David. *The Future of Marriage.* New York: Encounter, 2007.

Boccia, Maria L., et al. "Parental Divorce in Childhood Is Related to Lower Urinary Oxytocin Concentrations in Adulthood." *Journal of Comparative Psychology* 135 (2021) 74–81.

Brake, Elizabeth. "Marriage and Domestic Partnership." *Stanford Encyclopedia of Philosophy Archive,* July 14, 2021. Edited by Edward N. Zalta and Uri Nodelman. https://plato.stanford.edu/archives/win2023/entries/marriage.

Brandwein, Sharon. "Forty-Five Funny Wedding Vows to Exchange during Your Ceremony." *Brides,* Aug. 21, 2023. https://www.brides.com/funny-wedding-vows-5185364.

Britt-Lutter, Sonya, et al. "The Financial Implications of Cohabitation among Young Adults." *Journal of Financial Planning* 31 (2018) 38–45.

Brown, Susan L. "Family Structure and Child Well-Being: The Significance of Parental Cohabitation." *Journal of Marriage and Family* 66 (2004) 351–67. https://doi.org/10.1111/j.1741-3737.2004.00025.x.

———. "Marriage and Child Well-Being: Research and Policy Perspectives." *Journal of Marriage and Family* (2010) 1059–77. https://doi.org/10.1111/j.1741-3737.2010.00750.x.

Canadian Institute of Public Opinion. "Majority, under Thirty, Approve Trial Marriages." Press release, July 21, 1976.

———. "Under Thirty, Trial Marriages Approved by 4 to 5 Ratio." Press release, Aug. 11, 1971.

Cardus. "The Canadian Marriage Map." *Cardus,* June 23, 2020. Updated Aug. 2022. https://www.cardus.ca/research/the-canadian-marriage-map.

Caton, Carol L. M., et al. "Risk Factors for Homelessness among Indigent Urban Adults with No History of Psychotic Illness: A Case-Control Study." *American Journal of Public Health* 90 (2000) 258–63. https://doi.org/10.2105/AJPH.90.2.258.

CBC. "Quebec Tables Bill on Rights of Unmarried Partners, Creating New 'Parental Union Regime.'" *CBC,* Mar. 27, 2024. https://www.cbc.ca/

news/canada/montreal/quebec-bill-56-tabled-unmarried-partners-parents-1.7157432.

Cherlin, Andrew, et al. "Effects of Divorce on Mental Health through the Life Course." *American Sociological Review* 63 (1998) 239–49. https://doi.org/10.2307/2657325.

Chesterton, G. K. "The Drift from Domesticity." In *Brave New Family: G. K. Chesterton on Men and Women, Children, Sex, Divorce, Marriage, and the Family*, edited by Alvaro de Silva, 53–61. San Francisco: Ignatius, 1990.

Clinton, Hillary Rodham. *It Takes a Village: And Other Lessons Children Teach Us*. New York: Simon & Schuster, 2006.

Cohen, Rhaina. *The Other Significant Others: Reimagining Life with Friendship at the Center*. New York: St. Martin's, 2024.

Coontz, Stephanie. *Marriage, a History: How Love Conquered Marriage*. Annotated ed. New York: Penguin, 2006.

Corvino, John, and Maggie Gallagher. *Debating Same-Sex Marriage*. Point/Counterpoint. Oxford: Oxford University Press, 2012.

Crowe, Cameron, dir. *Jerry Maguire*. Culver City, CA: Sony, 1996.

Cruz, Julissa. *Marriage: More than a Century of Change*. National Center for Family and Marriage Research, 2013. https://www.bgsu.edu/content/dam/BGSU/college-of-arts-and-sciences/NCFMR/documents/FP/FP-13-13.pdf.

Department of Justice. "Selected Statistics on Canadian Families and Family Law: Second Edition." *Government of Canada*, Mar. 29, 2002. Rev. Dec. 28, 2022. https://www.justice.gc.ca/eng/rp-pr/fl-lf/famil/stat2000/f10_3.html.

Diamant, Jeff, et al. "What the Data Says about Abortion in the US." *Pew Research Center*, May 27, 2022. Updated Mar. 25, 2024. https://www.pewresearch.org/short-reads/2023/01/11/what-the-data-says-about-abortion-in-the-u-s-2.

Diekmann, Andreas, and Kurt Schmidheiny. "The Intergenerational Transmission of Divorce: A Fifteen-Country Study with the Fertility and Family Survey." *ETH Zurich Sociology Working Paper* 4 (2008) 1–24. https://www.researchgate.net/publication/5020712_The_Intergenerational_Transmission_of_Divorce_A_Fifteen-Country_Study_with_the_Fertility_and_Family_Survey.

Doherty, Maggie. "What Kate Did." *New Republic*, Mar. 23, 2016. https://newrepublic.com/article/131897/kate-millett-sexual-politics.

Douglas, Kristen. "Divorce Law in Canada." *Government of Canada*, Mar. 27, 2001. https://publications.gc.ca/Collection-R/LoPBdP/CIR/963-e.htm.

Dutton, Donald G., and Tonia L. Nicholls. "The Gender Paradigm in Domestic Violence Research and Theory: Part 1—The Conflict of Theory and Data." *Aggression and Violent Behavior* 10 (2005) 680–714.

Eberstadt, Mary. *Adam and Eve after the Pill: Paradoxes of the Sexual Revolution*. San Francisco: Ignatius, 2012.

BIBLIOGRAPHY

———. *How the West Really Lost God: A New Theory of Secularization*. West Conshohocken, PA: Templeton, 2013.

———. *Primal Screams: How the Sexual Revolution Created Identity Politics*. West Conshohocken, PA: Templeton, 2019.

Eberstadt, Nicholas. "Family Structure and the Decline of Work for Men in Postwar America." In *Unequal Family Lives: Causes and Consequences in Europe and the Americas*, edited by Naomi R. Cahn et al., 105–40. Cambridge: Cambridge University Press, 2018. https://www.cambridge.org/core/books/unequal-family-lives/family-structure-and-the-decline-of-work-for-men-in-postwar-america/4E987CC2E3C92509305092B4E44C1C2F.

Emba, Christine. *Rethinking Sex: A Provocation*. New York: Sentinel, 2022.

Frum, David. *How We Got Here: The 70's; The Decade That Brought You Modern Life—for Better or Worse*. Toronto: Vintage Canada, 2001.

Gairdner, William D. *The War against the Family: A Parent Speaks Out*. Toronto: Stoddart, 1993.

Galt, Virginia. "The Changing Face of the Canadian Family." *University Affairs*, Dec. 5, 2012. https://www.universityaffairs.ca/features/feature-article/the-changing-face-of-the-canadian-family.

Gauvreau, Michael. *The Catholic Origins of Quebec's Quiet Revolution, 1931–1970*. McGill-Queen's Studies in the History of Religion 2.41. Montreal: McGill-Queen's University Press, 2005.

Goldberg, Jonah. *Suicide of the West: How the Rebirth of Tribalism, Populism, Nationalism, and Identity Politics Is Destroying American Democracy*. New York: Crown Forum, 2018.

———. "There's Something about Marriage." *Dispatch*, Feb. 22, 2024. https://thedispatch.com/podcast/remnant/theres-something-about-marriage.

Groussé, Marion, and Marion Leturcq. "More or Less Unmarried: The Impact of Legal Settings of Cohabitation on Labour Market Outcomes." *European Economic Review* 149 (2022). https://doi.org/10.1016/j.euroecorev.2022.104259.

Gryn, Thomas, et al. "Married Couple Households Made Up Most of Family Households." *United States Census Bureau*, May 25, 2023. https://www.census.gov/library/stories/2023/05/family-households-still-the-majority.html.

Haidt, Jonathan. "Why I'm Increasingly Worried about Boys, Too." *American Institute for Boys and Men*, Nov. 14, 2023. https://aibm.org/commentary/why-im-increasingly-worried-about-boys-too.

Hamplova, Dana, et al. "One Pot or Two Pot Strategies? Income Pooling in Married and Unmarried Households in Comparative Perspective." *Journal of Comparative Family Studies* 40 (2009) 355–85. https://www.jstor.org/stable/41604288.

Harrington, Mary. *Feminism against Progress*. Washington, DC: Regnery, 2023.

# BIBLIOGRAPHY

Heckman, James. "James Heckman on the Role of Families in Human Flourishing." By Katharine Stevens. *YouTube*, Feb. 5, 2021. From American Enterprise Institute. https://www.youtube.com/watch?v=bjr62nLvg6M.

Hemez, Paul, and Chanell Washington. "Percentage and Number of Children Living with Two Parents Has Dropped Since 1968." *United States Census Bureau*, Apr. 12, 2021. https://www.census.gov/library/stories/2021/04/number-of-children-living-only-with-their-mothers-has-doubled-in-past-50-years.html.

Henderson, Rob. *Troubled: A Memoir of Foster Care, Family, and Social Class.* New York City: Gallery, 2024.

Henrich, Joseph, et al. "The Puzzle of Monogamous Marriage." *Philosophical Transactions of the Royal Society B: Biological Sciences* 367 (2012) 657–69. https://doi.org/10.1098/rstb.2011.0290.

Herman, Daniel B., et al. "Adverse Childhood Experiences: Are They Risk Factors for Adult Homelessness?" *American Journal of Public Health* 87 (1997) 249–55. https://doi.org/10.2105/AJPH.87.2.249.

Horowitz, Juliana Menasce, et al. "Marriage and Cohabitation in the US." *Pew Research Center*, Nov. 6, 2019. https://www.pewresearch.org/social-trends/2019/11/06/marriage-and-cohabitation-in-the-u-s.

Hrdy, Sarah Blaffer. *Mother Nature: A History of Mothers, Infants, and Natural Selection.* New York: Pantheon, 1999.

Hughes, Mary Elizabeth, and Linda J. Waite. "Marital Biography and Health at Mid-Life." *Journal of Health and Social Behavior* 50 (2009) 344–58. https://www.ncbi.nlm.nih.gov/pmc/articles/PMC3148098.

Hurst, Kiley. "Rising Share of Americans See Women Raising Children on Their Own, Cohabitation as Bad for Society." *Pew Research Center*, Mar. 11, 2022. https://www.pewresearch.org/short-reads/2022/03/11/rising-share-of-americans-see-women-raising-children-on-their-own-cohabitation-as-bad-for-society.

Hymowitz, Kay S. *Marriage and Caste in America: Separate and Unequal Families in a Post-Marital Age.* Chicago: Dee, 2007.

Institute for Family Studies. "Better-Educated Women Still Prefer Higher-Earning Husbands." *Institute for Family Studies*, Nov. 7, 2016. https://ifstudies.org/blog/better-educated-women-still-prefer-higher-earning-husbands.

Johnson, Sue. *Love Sense: The Revolutionary New Science of Romantic Relationships.* New York: Little, Brown, 2013.

Kearney, Melissa S. *The Two-Parent Privilege: How Americans Stopped Getting Married and Started Falling Behind.* Chicago: University of Chicago Press, 2023.

Kenney, Catherine T., and Sara S. McLanahan. "Why Are Cohabiting Relationships More Violent Than Marriages?" *Demography* 43 (2006) 127–40.

Kim, Young-Il, and Jeffrey Dew. "Religion and Volunteering in Marital Relationships." *Review of Religious Research* 61 (2019) 323–40. https://doi.org/10.1007/s13644-019-00382-1.

King, Kathleen B., and Harry T. Reis. "Marriage and Long-Term Survival after Coronary Artery Bypass Grafting." *Health Psychology* 31 (2012) 55–62. https://doi.org/10.1037/a0025061.

Koegel, Paul, et al. "Childhood Risk Factors for Homelessness among Homeless Adults." *American Journal of Public Health* 85 (1995) 1642–49. https://doi.org/10.2105/AJPH.85.12.1642.

Kotkin, Joel, et al. *The Rise of Post-Familialism: Humanity's Future?* Edited by Zina Klapper. Singapore: Civil Service College, 2012. https://www.newgeography.com/files/The%20Rise%20of%20Post-Familialism%20(ISBN9789810738976).pdf.

Kramer, Stephanie. "US Has World's Highest Rate of Children Living in Single-Parent Households." *Pew Research Center*, Dec. 12, 2019. https://www.pewresearch.org/short-reads/2019/12/12/u-s-children-more-likely-than-children-in-other-countries-to-live-with-just-one-parent.

Kreider, Rose M. "Living Arrangements of Children: 2004." *US Census Bureau*, Feb. 2008. Report P70-114. https://www.census.gov/library/publications/2008/demo/p70-114.html.

Krongrad, Arnon, et al. "Marriage and Mortality in Prostate Cancer." *Journal of Urology* 156 (1996) 1696–1700. https://doi.org/10.1016/S0022-5347(01)65485-5.

Lammintausta, Aino, et al. "Prognosis of Acute Coronary Events Is Worse in Patients Living Alone: The FINAMI Myocardial Infarction Register." *European Journal of Preventive Cardiology* 21 (2014) 989–96. https://doi.org/10.1177/2047487313475893.

Larson, Vicki. "Why All Women Need Renewable Marriage Contracts." *Medium*, Oct. 15, 2022. https://omgchronicles.medium.com/why-all-women-need-renewable-marriage-contracts-1ce134c89890.

Le Bourdais, Céline, and Évelyne Lapierre-Adamcyk. "Changes in Conjugal Life in Canada: Is Cohabitation Progressively Replacing Marriage?" *Journal of Marriage and Family* 66 (2004) 929–42. https://www.jstor.org/stable/3600167.

Lee, Barrett A., and Christopher J. Schreck. "Danger on the Streets: Marginality and Victimization among Homeless People." *American Behavioral Scientist* 48 (2005) 1055–81. https://doi.org/10.1177/0002764204274200.

Lewis, C. S. *The Joyful Christian: 127 Readings*. New York: Simon and Schuster, 1996.

Lincà, Léopold. *Le grand guide du mariage civil au Québec: Votre mariage civil au Québec de A à Z*. Quebec: Bibliothèque et Archives Nationales du Québec, 2021. https://www.notaire-mariage-civil.ca/wp-content/uploads/LE-GRAND-GUIDE-DU-MARIAGE-CIVIL-AU-QUEBEC-_-Votre-mariage-civil-de-A-a-Z-_Leopold-Linca-Notaire-2.pdf.

MacDonald, Michael. "Three Adults in Polyamorous Relationship Declared Legal Parents by N. L. Court." *CBC*, June 14, 2018. https://www.cbc.ca/news/canada/newfoundland-labrador/polyamourous-relationship-three-parents-1.4706560.

Macfarlane, Alan. *Marriage and Love in England: Modes of Reproduction 1300–1840*. Oxford: Blackwell, 1987.

Malvern, Paul. "Falling from Grace: The Rise and Fall of the Quebec Catholic Church." *LinkedIn*, May 30, 2023. https://www.linkedin.com/pulse/falling-from-grace-rise-fall-quebec-catholic-church-paul-malvern.

Martinuk, Susan. "Marriage Is Good for Your Health." *Cardus*, Sept. 29, 2016. https://www.cardus.ca/research/family/reports/marriage-is-good-for-your-health.

McGinn, Dave. "Single Parents Struggle as Canada's Policies Stay Stuck in the Age of Nuclear Families." *Globe and Mail*, Mar. 21, 2024. https://www.theglobeandmail.com/canada/article-single-parents-finances-policy.

McKay, John. "Confusion on the Hill." In *Divorcing Marriage: Unveiling the Dangers in Canada's New Social Experiment*, edited by Daniel Cere and Douglas Farrow, 29–38. Montreal: McGill-Queen's University Press, 2004.

McLanahan, Sara, and Gary D. Sandefur. *Growing Up with a Single Parent: What Hurts, What Helps*. Rev. ed. Cambridge, MA: Harvard University Press, 1997.

Menard, France-Pascale. "What Makes It Fall Apart? The Determinants of the Dissolution of Marriages and Common-Law Unions in Canada." *McGill Sociological Review* 2 (2011) 59–77. https://www.mcgill.ca/msr/volume2/article4.

Milke, Mark. "Missing Family Dynamics: Canadian Discussions about Family Fracturing, Poverty, and Inequality." *Cardus*, Sept. 11, 2017. https://www.cardus.ca/research/work-economics/reports/missing-family-dynamics.

Mitchell, Peter Jon. "Canadian Children at Home: Living Arrangements in the 2021 Census." *Cardus*, 2023. https://www.cardus.ca/research/family/reports/canadian-children-at-home-living-arrangements-in-the-2021-census.

———. *Canadian Millennials and the Value of Marriage*. Cardus, Aug. 24, 2016. https://www.cardus.ca/research/family/reports/canadian-millennials-and-the-value-of-marriage.

———. *Growing Up Married, Growing Up Common-Law*. Ottawa: Institute of Marriage and Family Canada, 2009. https://www.imfcanada.org/sites/default/files/Growing_up_married_common-law_FINAL.pdf.

———. "Living La Vida Lonely." *Cardus*, Nov. 12, 2018. https://www.cardus.ca/research/family/reports/living-la-vida-lonely.

Mitchell, Peter Jon, and Philip Cross. "The Marriage Gap between Rich and Poor Canadians." *Institute of Marriage and Family Canada*, Feb. 25, 2014. https://www.cardus.ca/research/family/articles/the-marriage-gap-between-rich-and-poor-canadians.

## BIBLIOGRAPHY

Mitchell, Peter Jon, and Lita L. Day. "For Love or Money? Why Partnered Young Adults Marry... or Don't." *Cardus*, Oct. 21, 2021. https://www.cardus.ca/research/family/reports/for-love-or-money.

Moore, Kristin A., et al. *Marriage from a Child's Perspective: How Does Family Structure Affect Children, and What Can We Do about It?* Washington, DC: Child Trends, 2002. Research brief. https://cms.childtrends.org/wp-content/uploads/2002/06/MarriageRB602.pdf.

Morin, Rich. "Is Divorce Contagious?" *Pew Research Center*, Oct. 21, 2013. https://www.pewresearch.org/short-reads/2013/10/21/is-divorce-contagious.

Morse, Jennifer Roback. *Love and Economics: Why the Laissez-Faire Family Doesn't Work*. Dallas: Spence, 2004.

Neufeld, Gordon, and Gabor Maté. *Hold On to Your Kids: Why Parents Need to Matter More Than Peers*. Toronto: Vintage Canada, 2004.

Neuman, Mark D., and Rachel M. Werner. "Marital Status and Postoperative Functional Recovery." *JAMA Surgery* 151 (2016) 194–96. https://doi.org/10.1001/jamasurg.2015.3240.

Newport, Frank. "Untangling Americans' Complex Views of Morality." *Gallup*, June 17, 2022. https://news.gallup.com/opinion/polling-matters/393782/untangling-americans-complex-views-morality.aspx.

Nichols, Elizabeth M. "Marital Status Is an Independent Predictor of Survival for Patients Undergoing Definitive Chemoradiation for Stage III Non-Small Cell Lung Cancer." Supplement, *Journal of Thoracic Oncology* 14 (2012) S203–40.

Nock, Steven L. "A Comparison of Marriages and Cohabiting Relationships." *Journal of Family Issues* 16 (1995) 53–76. https://doi.org/10.1177/019251395016001004.

Obama, Barack. "Text of Obama's Fatherhood Speech." *Politico*, June 15, 2008. https://www.politico.com/story/2008/06/text-of-obamas-fatherhood-speech-011094.

Perry, Louise. *The Case against the Sexual Revolution: A New Guide to Sex in the Twenty-First Century*. Cambridge: Polity, 2022.

———. "The Modern Dating Catastrophe, Sex Recession & Population Collapse." *YouTube*, Apr. 24, 2024. From *Triggernometry*. https://www.youtube.com/watch?v=6nMsexC-a4Y.

Pinquart, Martin, and Paul R. Duberstein. "Associations of Social Networks with Cancer Mortality: A Meta-Analysis." *Critical Reviews in Oncology/Hematology* 75 (2010) 122–37. https://doi.org/10.1016/j.critrevonc.2009.06.003.

Pippert, Timothy D. *Road Dogs and Loners: Family Relationships among Homeless Men*. Washington, DC: Lexington, 2007.

Popenoe, David. *Life without Father: Compelling New Evidence That Fatherhood and Marriage Are Indispensable for the Good of Children and Society*. New York: Free Press, 1996.

Proulx, Christine M., et al. "Marital Quality and Personal Well-Being: A Meta-Analysis." *Journal of Marriage and Family* 69 (2007) 576–93. https://doi.org/10.1111/j.1741-3737.2007.00393.x.

Putnam, Robert D. *Bowling Alone: The Collapse and Revival of American Community.* New York: Simon & Schuster, 2000.

Reeves, Richard V. *Of Boys and Men: Why the Modern Male Is Struggling, Why It Matters, and What to Do about It.* Washington, DC: Brookings Institution, 2022.

Reeves, Richard V., and Christopher Pulliam. "Middle Class Marriage Is Declining, and Likely Deepening Inequality." *Brookings Institution*, Mar. 11, 2020. https://www.brookings.edu/research/middle-class-marriage-is-declining-and-likely-deepening-inequality.

Romo, Rafael. "Mexican Legislator Proposes 2-Year Marriage Dissolution Option." *CNN*, Oct. 4, 2011. https://www.cnn.com/2011/10/03/world/americas/mexico-2-year-marriages/index.html.

Rosenfeld, Michael J., and Katharina Roesler. "Cohabitation Experience and Cohabitation's Association with Marital Dissolution." *Journal of Marriage and Family* 81 (2019) 42–58. https://doi.org/10.1111/jomf.12530.

Ross, Catherine E., and John Mirowsky. "Parental Divorce, Life-Course Disruption and Adult Depression." *Journal of Marriage and Family* 61 (1999) 1034–45. https://doi.org/10.2307/354022.

Santos-Longhurst, Adrienne. "Why Is Oxytocin Known as the 'Love Hormone'? And 11 Other FAQs." *Healthline*, July 12, 2023. https://www.healthline.com/health/love-hormone.

Schoenborn, Charlotte A. "Marital Status and Health: United States, 1999–2002." *Advance Data* 351 (2004) 1–32.

Sedlak, A. J., et al. *Fourth National Incidence Study of Child Abuse and Neglect (NIS-4): Report to Congress.* Washington, DC: US Department of Health and Human Services, Administration for Children and Families, 2010. https://www.acf.hhs.gov/opre/report/fourth-national-incidence-study-child-abuse-and-neglect-nis-4-report-congress.

Smith, Jesse, and Nicholas H. Wolfinger. "Re-Examining the Link between Premarital Sex and Divorce." *Journal of Family Issues* 45 (2024) 674–96. https://doi.org/10.1177/0192513X231155673.

Sommers, Christina Hoff. *Freedom Feminism: Its Surprising History and Why It Matters Today.* Washington, DC: AEI, 2013.

Stack, Steven, and J. Ross Eshleman. "Marital Status and Happiness: A 17-Nation Study." *Journal of Marriage and Family* 60 (1998) 527–36. https://doi.org/10.2307/353867.

Stanley, Scott M., and Galena K. Rhoades. *What's the Plan? Cohabitation, Engagement, and Divorce.* Charlottesville, VA: Institute for Family Studies, 2023. https://ifstudies.org/ifs-admin/resources/reports/cohabitationreportapr2023-final.pdf.

Stanley, Scott M., et al. "Sliding versus Deciding: Inertia and the Premarital Cohabitation Effect." *Family Relations* 55 (2006) 499–509.

## BIBLIOGRAPHY

Statistics Canada. "Census Family." *Statistics Canada*, Nov. 15, 2015. Updated Aug. 20, 2019. https://www23.statcan.gc.ca/imdb/p3Var.pl?Function=UnitI&Id=27666.

———. "Census Profile, 2021 Census of Population." *Statistics Canada*, Feb. 9, 2022. Updated Nov. 15, 2023. https://www12.statcan.gc.ca/census-recensement/2021/dp-pd/prof/index.cfm?Lang=E.

———. "Disaggregated Trends in Poverty from the 2021 Census of Population." *Statistics Canada*, Nov. 9, 2022. https://www12.statcan.gc.ca/census-recensement/2021/as-sa/98-200-X/2021009/98-200-X2021009-eng.cfm#.

———. "A Fifty-Year Look at Divorces in Canada, 1970 to 2020." *Statistics Canada*, Mar. 9, 2022. https://www150.statcan.gc.ca/n1/daily-quotidien/220309/dq220309a-eng.htm.

———. "Gender Diversity Status of Couple Family, Type of Union and Presence of Children: Canada, Provinces and Territories, Census Metropolitan Areas and Census Agglomerations." *Statistics Canada*, July 13, 2022. Table 98-10-0136-01. https://www150.statcan.gc.ca/t1/tbl1/en/tv.action?pid=9810013601.

———. "How Many Children in Canada Have Experienced the Separation or Divorce of Their Parents? Results from the 2019 Canadian Health Survey on Children and Youth." *Statistics Canada*, Mar. 23, 2022. https://www150.statcan.gc.ca/n1/pub/11-627-m/11-627-m2022018-eng.htm.

———. "Live Births, by Marital Status of Mother." *Statistics Canada*, Sept. 26, 2023. Table 13-10-0419-01 (formerly CANSIM 102-4506). https://www150.statcan.gc.ca/t1/tbl1/en/cv.action?pid=1310041901.

———. "Lone-Parent Families: The New Face of an Old Phenomenon." *Statistics Canada*, Feb. 16, 2015. https://www150.statcan.gc.ca/n1/pub/11-630-x/11-630-x2015002-eng.htm.

———. "Number of Divorces and Divorce Indicators." *Statistics Canada*, Nov. 14, 2022. Table 39-10-0051-01. https://www150.statcan.gc.ca/t1/tbl1/en/tv.action?pid=3910005101.

———. "State of the Union: Canada Leads the G7 with Nearly One-Quarter of Couples Living Common Law, Driven by Quebec." *Statistics Canada*, July 13, 2022. https://www150.statcan.gc.ca/n1/daily-quotidien/220713/dq220713b-eng.htm.

Stone, Lyman. "Does Getting Married Really Make You Happier?" *Institute for Family Studies*, Feb. 7, 2022. https://ifstudies.org/blog/does-getting-married-really-make-you-happier.

———. "How Many Kids Do Women Want?" *Institute for Family Studies*, June 1, 2018. https://ifstudies.org/blog/how-many-kids-do-women-want.

———. "She's (Not) Having a Baby: Why Half of Canadian Women Are Falling Short of Their Fertility Desires." *Cardus*, Jan. 31, 2023. https://www.cardus.ca/research/family/reports/she-s-not-having-a-baby.

Stone, Lyman, and Spencer James. *Marriage Still Matters: Demonstrating the Link between Marriage and Fertility in the Twenty-First Century.*

Charlottesville, VA: Institute for Family Studies, 2023. https://ifstudies.org/ifs-admin/resources/reports/marriagestillmatters-final.pdf.

Straus, Murray. "Thirty Years of Denying the Evidence on Gender Symmetry in Partner Violence: Implications for Prevention and Treatment." *Partner Abuse* 1 (2010) 332–62.

Stuart, Jo. "How Family Status and Life Cycle Events Affect Volunteering." *NCVO*, Sept. 18, 2019. https://www.ncvo.org.uk/news-and-insights/news-index/the-links-between-family-and-volunteering-a-review-of-the-evidence/how-family-status-and-life-cycle-events-affect-volunteering.

Taylor-Coleman, Jasmine. "Polyamorous Marriage: Is There a Future for Three-Way Weddings?" *BBC*, July 20, 2017. https://www.bbc.com/news/world-40655103.

Thornberry, Terence P., et al. "Family Disruption and Delinquency." *Office of Juvenile Justice and Delinquency Prevention: Juvenile Justice Bulletin*, Sept. 1999. https://www.ojp.gov/pdffiles1/ojjdp/178285.pdf.

Trinko, Katrina. "Dating Crisis Fuels Marriage Crisis." *Daily Signal*, Feb. 13, 2024. https://www.dailysignal.com/2024/02/13/want-more-marriages-make-dating-less-brutal.

United States Census Bureau. "American Community Survey 1-Year Data (2005–2022)." *United States Census Bureau*, Sept. 14, 2023. https://www.census.gov/data/developers/data-sets/acs-1year.html.

———. "Census Bureau Releases New Estimates on America's Families and Living Arrangements." *United States Census Bureau*, Nov. 17, 2022. Press Release Number CB22-TPS.99. https://www.census.gov/newsroom/press-releases/2022/americas-families-and-living-arrangements.html.

———. *Median Age at First Marriage: 1890 to Present*. United States Census Bureau 2023. Figure MS-2. https://www.census.gov/content/dam/Census/library/visualizations/time-series/demo/families-and-households/ms-2.pdf.

University of Maryland Medical Center. "Married Lung Cancer Patients Survive Longer than Single Patients After Treatment." *Science Daily*, Sept. 6, 2012. https://www.sciencedaily.com/releases/2012/09/120906092803.htm.

University of Ottawa Heart Institute. "Healing Hearts Together." *University of Ottawa Heart Institute*, n.d. https://www.ottawaheart.ca/researchers/clinical-trials/healing-hearts-together.

Van Maren, Jonathon. "How Porn Is Ruining the Lives of Men and Making Them Miserable." *Bridgehead*, Oct. 13, 2020. https://thebridgehead.ca/2020/10/13/how-porn-is-ruining-the-lives-of-men-and-making-them-miserable.

Vlosky, Denese Ashbaugh, and Pamela A. Monroe. "The Effective Dates of No-Fault Divorce Laws in the Fifty States." *Family Relations* 51 (2002) 317–24. http://www.jstor.org/stable/3700329.

Waite, Linda, and Maggie Gallagher. *The Case for Marriage: Why Married People Are Happier, Healthier, and Better Off Financially*. New York: Broadway, 2001.

## BIBLIOGRAPHY

Wallerstein, Judith S., et al. *The Unexpected Legacy of Divorce: The Twenty-Five Year Landmark Study*. New York: Hachette, 2001.

Wang, Li, et al. "Marital Status and Colon Cancer Outcomes in US Surveillance, Epidemiology, and End Results Registries: Does Marriage Affect Cancer Survival by Gender and Stage?" *Cancer Epidemiology* 35 (2011) 417–22. https://doi.org/10.1016/j.canep.2011.02.004.

Wang, Wendy. "The US Divorce Rate Has Hit a Fifty-Year Low." *Institute for Family Studies*, Nov. 10, 2020. https://ifstudies.org/blog/the-us-divorce-rate-has-hit-a-50-year-low.

Wang, Wendy, and Brad Wilcox. *The Power of the Success Sequence for Disadvantaged Young Adults*. Charlottesville, VA: Institute for Family Studies, 2022. https://www.aei.org/wp-content/uploads/2022/05/success sequencedisadvantagedya-final.pdf?x91208.

Wilcox, Brad. "For as Long as Our Love Shall Last: How the Soulmate Myth Makes Marriage Less Stable and Less Happy." *Institute for Family Studies*, May 20, 2020. https://ifstudies.org/blog/for-as-long-as-our-love-shall-last-how-the-soulmate-myth-makes-marriage-less-stable-and-less-happy.

———. *Get Married: Why Americans Must Defy the Elites, Forge Strong Families, and Save Civilization*. New York: Broadside, 2024.

———. "Marriage Makes Our Children Richer. Here's Why." *Atlantic*, Oct. 29, 2013. https://www.theatlantic.com/business/archive/2013/10/marriage-makes-our-children-richer-heres-why/280930.

Wilcox, Brad. *See also* Wilcox, W. Bradford.

Wilcox, Brad, and Chris Bullivant. "The American Dream Can Be Achieved If We Spend More Time Building Strong, Stable Families." *USA Today*, May 20, 2022. https://www.usatoday.com/story/opinion/columnist/2022/05/20/american-family-families-disparities/9722599002.

Wilcox, W. Bradford. "The Evolution of Divorce." *National Affairs* 60 (2009). https://www.nationalaffairs.com/publications/detail/the-evolution-of-divorce.

———. "When Marriage Disappears: The Retreat from Marriage in Middle America." In *When Marriage Disappears: The New Middle America*, edited by W. Bradford Wilcox and Elizabeth Marquardt, 13–60. New York: Broadway, 2011. https://fatherhoodchannel.com/wp-content/uploads/2010/12/when-marriage-disappears.pdf.

Wilcox, W. Bradford. *See also* Wilcox, Brad.

Wilcox, W. Bradford, and Jeffrey Dew. "Is Love a Flimsy Foundation? Soulmate Versus Institutional Models of Marriage." Special issue, *Social Science Research* 39 (2010) 687–99. https://doi.org/10.1016/j.ssresearch.2010.05.006.

Wilcox, W. Bradford, and Elizabeth Marquardt, eds. *When Marriage Disappears: The New Middle America*. New York: Broadway, 2011. https://fatherhoodchannel.com/wp-content/uploads/2010/12/when-marriage-disappears.pdf.

Wilcox, Brad, and Wendy Wang. "The Marriage Divide: How and Why Working-Class Families Are More Fragile Today." *Institute for Family Studies*, Sept. 25, 2017. https://ifstudies.org/blog/the-marriage-divide-how-and-why-working-class-families-are-more-fragile-today.

———. "Who Is Happiest? Married Mothers and Fathers, per the Latest General Social Survey." *Institute for Family Studies*, Sept. 12, 2023. https://ifstudies.org/blog/who-is-happiest-married-mothers-and-fathers-per-the-latest-general-social-survey.

Wilcox, W. Bradford, and Nicholas H. Wolfinger. *Men & Marriage: Debunking the Ball and Chain Myth*. Charlottesville, VA: Institute for Family Studies, 2017. https://ifstudies.org/ifs-admin/resources/men-and-marriage-research-brief.pdf.

Williams, David R., et al. "Marital Status and Psychiatric Disorders among Blacks and Whites." *Journal of Health and Social Behavior* 33 (1992) 140–57.

Willingham, Emily. "People Have Been Having Less Sex—Whether They're Teenagers or Forty-Somethings." *Scientific American*, Jan. 3, 2022. https://www.scientificamerican.com/article/people-have-been-having-less-sex-whether-theyre-teenagers-or-40-somethings.

Wilson, James Q. *The Marriage Problem: How Our Culture Has Weakened Families*. New York: Harper, 2003.

Witherspoon Institute. *Marriage and the Public Good: Ten Principles*. Princeton, NJ: Witherspoon Institute, 2008.

Wolfinger, Nicholas H. "Are Married People Still Happier?" *Institute for Family Studies*, May 28, 2019. https://ifstudies.org/blog/are-married-people-still-happier.

Wong, Chun Wai, et al. "Marital Status and Risk of Cardiovascular Diseases: A Systematic Review and Meta-Analysis." *Heart* [British Cardiac Society] 104 (2018) 1937–48. https://doi.org/10.1136/heartjnl-2018-313005.

Wu, Zheng, et al. "Family Structure and University Enrollment and Completion." Paper presented at the Population Association of America, San Francisco, 2012. https://paa2012.populationassociation.org/papers/120858.

Yenor, Scott. *Family Politics: The Idea of Marriage in Modern Political Thought*. Waco: Baylor University Press, 2012.

Young, Katherine, and Paul Nathanson. "Keep It All in the Family." *Globe and Mail*, May 2, 2003. https://www.theglobeandmail.com/opinion/keep-it-all-in-the-family/article750274.

www.ingramcontent.com/pod-product-compliance
Lightning Source LLC
Chambersburg PA
CBHW020856160426
43192CB00007B/951